Adventure Available

Discovering Life with an Extravagantly
Loving God

By

Margaret Grady Turner

United Ink Media
A Ministry of United Assembly
Seneca, South Carolina
www.unitedassembly.com

In loving memory of A.J. Buffington and Brittani Panozzo

Though you did not live long enough to see your thirtieth birthdays, you lived your lives with a beautiful devotion to our Savior, love for others, and an inspiring pursuit of justice here on earth. You are missed every day.

Special Thanks

❖

To my friends Natalie Stover, Cathy Roper, Randi Owens, A.J. Zeilstra, and Sharon Carnahan for their contributions to this work.

To my amazing husband, Rick, for offering his creative feedback, supporting me throughout the entire process, and empowering me every day to use my gifts to edify God's Kingdom.

And finally to my mom and editor, Deborah Grady, for the many hours she devoted to shaping my words for greater clarity, and for teaching me how to read and write while imparting the love of it as well.

Table of Contents

❖

CHAPTER 1

The Greatest Adventure

I came dangerously close to not finishing college. By that I don't mean that I thought about dropping out to try and make it as a rock star—or that I lacked the academic drive to get to my classes or do my work. In the first few weeks of my freshman year of college I almost died. Four crazy guys named Austin, Brent, John and Rick decided that it would be a good idea to go to West Virginia during Fall Break and go white water rafting on the second most dangerous rapids in the continental United States. Because I enjoyed hanging out with them so much, I accepted their invitation to join them on this risky trip.

Our guide told us emphatically as we approached a category V+ rapid—ironically named *Insignificant*—to make sure we stayed in the raft while navigating this one, as he had actually seen folks die underneath this section's enormous undercut rock. He told us he knew a couple on their honeymoon that fell out of their raft on this particular rapid. They went under holding hands and never came back up. *Awesome story,* I thought sarcastically. Perhaps the cheesiness of the story detracted from the seriousness of the warning. Category V+ meant that it was for experts and I had only rafted once or twice before.

When our raft crashed into a hydraulic wave and I was thrown into the near freezing water, I went under. I went under for a long time. I remember my chest burning, as I had not held my breath for that long in the history of my life. In fact, I was under so long I remember thinking, *God, I know you're not finished with me yet, but holy mountain man, this is a really long time to be trapped under water.* After this frantic conversation with my Maker, my male companions spotted me as I emerged from the cold river and pulled me back into the raft. I must have lain limp for several minutes completely wiped out. Then when I felt replenished with oxygen I thought, without any hint of sarcasm, *that was awesome! I'm so glad I did not stick around the residence hall during break.*

At eighteen years old, I lived to tell about my near death experience and laugh about it. But I did not *just* get a second chance at breathing oxygen that trip, I also got reacquainted with the Giver of Life. My four new friends and our male chaperone stayed in a quite large tent while I, the only girl, stayed in the most pitiful one-person tent. The evening after my encounter with the raging river, I wrapped up in my twenty-below-zero sleeping bag and I sobbed as it snowed outside, hoping the guys did not hear me. I told God I regretted ignoring Him my first few months in college. I told Him I missed Him. I told Him I hadn't forgotten that He chased me. I told Him I wanted to be close again.

You see, this was not the first time I had almost died from drowning, figuratively speaking. I grew up in a Christian home, with loving Christian parents who took me to a loving Christian church. But when seventh grade rolled around I told my parents I wanted to go to public school instead of being home-schooled by my mom, and they listened. And for a year I barely stayed afloat. Kids made fun of me. Of course, no one could blame them. I had braces and a bowl haircut. I wore hand-me-downs that were no longer in style. I did not know any songs by The Backstreet Boys or Nirvana.

Every night when I went to bed I doubted that God cared or He even existed. But I prayed habitually through my tears after being tucked in every night, "God if you are real, don't let go of me." And He didn't.

Not only did He not let me go, He chased me, He pursued me in the fiercely relentless way that only He can. He chased me because I belonged to Him. He chased me because He ached, even longed to bring home His baby girl. Caught in the rapids of teenage turmoil, He replaced my breathless being with life. He pursued me so passionately that one night at a Wednesday night service, in a moment of pure desperation, I went to the altar for prayer. I wept as a high-school student laid hands on me, praying silently. Though this older girl did not know me well, and certainly did not know the agony I endured each day in school, or the pleas I prayed each night, she took the time to hear from our Heavenly Father on my behalf. After a significant period of silence, she said, "God is never going to let go of you." Hearing the confirmation I had been longing for changed me forever. And He hasn't let go of me. Not once.

Though that first rescue had temporarily faded in memory, I could not ignore this second rescue. I decided that night in West Virginia that I wanted to live close to Jesus. The adrenaline of the day did not compare to the Holy Spirit stirring in my heart. God created me for relationship with Him and others. Those relationship adventures far exceeded rafting the raging rapids of the Gauley River. I could not bear the thought of a normal life, or a safe life, or a specifically calculated path. I wanted excitement, mystery, and a can't-quite-catch-your-breath spontaneity. I wanted a life bigger than just me. I wanted to live in a way that tangibly revealed a loving, gracious, absolutely good, powerful God. On the brink of the most critical decade of my life, I partnered with Christ, and living side-by-side with Him has changed everything.

Saying yes to His invitation to join and run this race with Him is the best, most beautiful way to run your life. Though the invitation to do life with the Father, Son, and Holy Spirit is always extended to you, no matter what your age, there is no better time to accept it than in your twenties. There is no decade with a more profound impact on your life. Here are just some of the things you'll likely be making decisions about:

- College
- Career
- Which friendships to invest the most in
- Developing diet and fitness habits
- Spending and saving money

- Who to date/marry

- Commitment to God

- Church involvement

Whether you make these decisions with or without Christ by your side makes a big difference, because these decisions impact everything else in your life. If you think it does not matter what you do with this decade and treat it like an extended adolescence, you may find yourself mourning rather than celebrating on your thirtieth birthday.

I'm not a fan of regret. And that's not because I'm afraid of making mistakes. It's because every failure Christ has turned into a teaching moment. If I could go back in time and do it differently, I wouldn't—I'm too excited about what is coming next. Christ can make all things new, and He can restore things that are lost or broken. Your twenties, in many respects, are the foundation for your adult life. When you build that foundation with Christ, you do not worry about cracks or imperfections— He's got you covered! You're just ready to see what is coming next, because you know it will be beautiful, and fun, and more satisfying that anything else available to you.

If you want to live the adventure, you've got to be willing to do things that scare you and things that are tough. My dad served as an editor of a Christian magazine for many years. He felt that God had more for him in store, but he gave God some conditions on what he would and would not do. To be specific, he told God he did not want to speak in public or get on airplanes, but other than that he remained open to what God might ask of him. Finally, after a time of resistance, he surrendered and prayed a scary prayer with no conditions, "Here am I Lord. Send me." Today he is a leader in the global movement against the oppression of women. He is partnering with people from Asia, South America, and Africa to open domestic violence shelters for women and homes for abandoned girls. He fights human trafficking, violence against women, and discrimination of women in our churches by raising awareness and challenging men to have the attitude of Jesus towards women. And yes, He speaks to crowds of thousands and gets on a plane several times each month. He knows what it means to partner with Christ, to serve on the front lines on issues that our Heavenly Father cares about so deeply. I can't imagine a world where he still refuses to get on airplanes. I'm sure even he could not count how many adventures he would have missed if he had kept himself limited to his conditions.

When I was just out of undergrad, my friend, Brittani, a senior ministry student, came to see me for some advice. She was entering her final semester of college and trying to decide if she should do her final internship abroad in Africa or if she should intern on campus and get one more semester with her friends. Without a bit of spiritual guidance, I responded confidently, "Brittani, you have your whole life to go to Africa. Enjoy one more semester on campus."

Brittani was the kind of young woman filled with compassion for the marginalized, oppressed, and poor. She was always getting involved in some type of social justice movement. She did not just have a desire to see a different corner of the world for sport. She wanted to change the world. Thankfully she ignored my advice and went to Africa. And a week after returning home, just days before she'd walk across the Swails Center stage at Emmanuel College and receive her college diploma, Brittani's life ended abruptly in a car accident.

And I still think about my advice to her. "You have your whole life to go to Africa."

When we lose people we love, people who make every second count, we reevaluate certain things. We get this beautiful sense of urgency about life and making our lives count for something bigger than ourselves. This urgency does not come from a sense of fear or anxiety, but out of the opportunity before us. Our lives matter. They matter to God and they matter to others. Each day we are given a chance to live in partnership with Christ and do something we could never do without Him.

When we think we have all the time in the world, we waste opportunities. We throw them away, because later is an all too appealing option. But when each day is a gift, we live with a certain intentionality and grace. There is no delay in making our lives count.

I think one of the greatest tragedies of our time is twenty-somethings living in an extended adolescence. An illusion that life does not really start until you turn thirty fools a lot of young people. We have this epidemic of twenty-somethings living in their parent's basement, racking up credit card debt, hooking up with whoever seems interested at the time, and postponing dreams because somehow we've believed the lie that this time does not really count. We've believed the lie that we have our whole lives to do whatever lies deep in our hearts.

Things are changing though. It is my hope that more and more men and women in their twenties will live like Brittani. Despite all the "you have your whole life to…." advice, they'll live with that beautiful urgency, follow the prompting of the Holy Spirit, and live each day with purpose and passion.

Maybe you have fears about the future. Maybe surrendering to God sounds absolutely terrifying. Maybe you think God is terrifying or mean or indifferent or just slightly disappointed with you for not being perfect, and that has kept you from fully and joyfully partnering with Him in this life. I can relate. In college I struggled with faith and partnership with Christ, because I lacked real, radiant revelation of the Triune God. But as I have discovered more and more of the true nature of our Heavenly Father, Jesus, and Holy Spirit, partnership together only becomes more beautiful, both safe and scary, and I would not have it any other way. He is love. He is good. He is a rescuer. I'm convinced that the greatest adventure available to us is one in deep, intimate relationship with the Heavenly Father, empowered by the Holy Spirit, and yoked with Christ as a partner in the ministry of reconciliation. I am also sure that living life with our extravagantly loving God, with the adventure available in Him, is the best way to make every day count.

Reflections

1. What are some of the hopes, dreams, and plans you have for your life?

2. Instead of telling yourself you have your whole life to do these things, what could you start doing today that will help you accomplish your life goals?

3. What part do you see God having in your life adventures? Do you see Him as a partner? A cheerleader? A critic? An apathetic bystander? Non-existent?

Meditation

Imagine the moment that God created you. As He carefully knit you together, what was He putting in your heart? Consider your longing for adventure, your ambitions, and your desire to live with purpose. Take a few moments to recognize that He made you with such passion for a purpose.

NOTES

ADVERTURE AVAILABLE

CHAPTER 2

❖

Dual Citizenship

My good friend Eric decided to take a group of middle school and high school students on a ministry trip to Peru. He asked me to co-lead the trip and I enthusiastically agreed. I traveled to Peru that summer and fell in love with everything about it. From the big city of Lima to the mountains of Limbatambo, everything about Peru left me breathless.

While traveling through Lima one day, we came across a woman in distress. Though I spoke Spanish pretty well, I could not make out what she kept asking of me. I immediately assumed she might be hungry and tried to give her a cereal bar from my pack. She refused. She looked desperate, so I found another leader who spoke Spanish fluently to see if she could figure out what the woman might need.

"She has been sick for a very long time and no one will touch her. She wants prayer," my friend whispered.

I put the granola bar down and embraced the woman. We held each other for what seemed like forever. She squeezed me tightly as you might embrace a friend you had not seen in a very long time. I don't remember praying for her. I just remember hoping she knew she was precious, loved, and not forgotten. I remember loving her, not because I knew anything specific about her, but because in that moment I felt how much Jesus loved her.

That experienced wrecked me for the rest of the day. I could not even talk to my teammates afterwards. I saw that encounter as bigger than just the two of us. I thought about the Church in the United States and those in need and wondered how often we throw a donation or a bag of rice or used unfashionable clothing or a cereal bar at those in need when they are crying out to be held, to be loved. I know meeting physical needs is very important. People who are hungry, thirsty for clean drinking water, or sick with disease cannot even process the good news while their physical bodies are suffering. We have to take care of people practically. But the good news is not a statement that can just be proclaimed and received. The good news is the tangible, real, felt love of Jesus and those who follow Him.

Life with our extravagantly loving God is a grand adventure. We have an opportunity to move from a vague desire to change the world to accept a specific incredible mission. When we live in community with our Heavenly Father, Jesus, and Holy Spirit, we are divinely encouraged and equipped to bring heaven here on earth. This is the driving purpose behind every Christian effort to promote social justice. When something on earth is not as it would be in heaven, we as partners with God are called to be a catalyst for change.

Poverty, racism, violence, discrimination, hopelessness, and fear do not exist in heaven. Thus we know as partners with Christ we can help transform situations by inviting heaven here on earth. We can help eradicate the darkness in our world. We can serve as agents of generosity, protection, equality, and justice. We can sow love, joy, peace, and hope. This is the real adventure we embark on when we enter into relationship with God. He has been up to this since the beginning. When we enter the family of God, we inherit the family business.

> *But because of his great love for us, God, who is rich in mercy, made us alive with Christ even when we were dead in transgressions—it is by grace you have been saved. And God raised us up with Christ and seated us with him in the heavenly realms in Christ Jesus, in order that in the coming ages he might show the incomparable riches of his grace, expressed in his kindness to us in Christ Jesus. For it is by grace you have been saved, through faith—and this is not from yourselves, it is the gift of God—not by works, so that no one can boast. For we are God's handiwork, created in Christ Jesus to do good works, which God prepared in advance for us to do.*

—EPHESIANS 2: 4–8

Accepting our reality as dual citizens of heaven and earth and all the authority that comes with being an heir with Christ is essential to understanding our calling. When we come into the family of God, essentially we are issued a second passport. While we roam about the earth, we are simultaneously seated with Christ in the heavens. Our position as those seated with Christ equips us for such good works all over the world.

This reality is difficult for many to grasp. Some of us have been conditioned to think of ourselves as simply workhorses. Some think God wants to use them, but they do not know how deeply loved they are, nor do they recognize or use the authority given to them. Thus we accept an incomplete picture of our calling to be salt and light, and we simply strive to do stuff for God. Of course we do things for Our Savior. But we do not just work on behalf of Christ—we work with Christ, side by side. Jesus gives us the perfect visual aid:

> *Come to me, all you who are weary and burdened, and I will give you rest. Take my yoke upon you and learn from me, for I am gentle and humble in heart, and you will find rest for your souls. For my yoke is easy and my burden is light.*

> —MATTHEW 11: 28–30

This passage in Matthew certainly deepens our understanding of what relationship and partnership with Him looks like. "My yoke is easy and my burden is light." When I hear the word "yoke," I immediately think about how I want my eggs over-easy, deliciously runny. But Jesus' friends lived before tractors and would have thought of a tool used to couple two animals working together on the same task. So yes, we do things for Christ and His Kingdom, but never without Him coupled with us, pulling the bulk of the weight. That is why He goes on to say you will have rest and supernatural peace. Doing something *for* God is stressful. Partnering *with* Christ for the same mission—knowing He'll pull most of the weight—is exciting. Calling never comes without divine equipping.

Again we are reminded that we are not alone. Christ is beside us and we are beside Him. We are seated with Christ in heavenly places. On the earth, in the adventure, Christ is side by side with us. We are never alone—we are always close to the Author of all good works—all meaningful expeditions.

Let's consider the parable of the Good Samaritan. Pastors and Christian leaders utilize this passage to invigorate others for Christian service, to inspire others to be that good neighbor. But Luke is strategic about the way he writes, so stories do not get put in any random order. What follows the story of the Good Samaritan? Our first encounter with Mary and Martha (see Luke 10: 30–42.) Martha is up to lots of productive work. Mary takes the position of a disciple, seated at Jesus' feet. Martha asks Jesus to get Mary busy, but Jesus says Mary has chosen what is a better priority. Luke pairs these stories together because of his understanding of human nature and his revelation of the heart of Christ. Be a good neighbor to all. Bring the Kingdom here on earth. But do not go it alone. Sit at His feet. Wear His yoke. For the former is impossible without the latter.

Whenever I talk about the woman in Peru, I cry. Ten years removed from her embrace, I still feel it all. I don't cry because I feel bad for her, or because I'm sad about the lack of solutions to the world's biggest social problems. I cry because I actually felt, and still feel, a glimpse of what the Heavenly Father feels for His children. That kind of love takes your breath away. That kind of love overwhelms to tears. The fact that Jesus poured out everything He had, endured separation from his loving Father, suffered every kind of pain we might ever encounter is half the story. He died on a cross in His mission to save us in every way that we need saving, and did not stop there. He conquered death, hell, and the grave. He destroyed the Evil One and everything not of the light. And every day He asks us to wear this yoke with Him, soliciting our help to bring home our lost brothers and sisters, bring hope to those in despair, to bring restoration and healing to those in need.

Jesus is our savior. Jesus is a friend that sticks closer than a brother. Jesus is Lord and King of our very lives. Jesus set us free for freedom's sake. Jesus is the way, the truth, the life, and the only way to the Father. And He is not far away. He is the vine, we are the branches, connected so intimately—we draw life from Him. Relationship with Jesus means closeness, partnership, and commonality with Jesus. Our position is a co-heir with Him. Our opportunity is to co-labor with Him on this ever so important mission to bring heaven here on earth.

Just as it is true that Jesus is yoked with us as we go about this adventure on Earth, we also sit with Christ in heavenly places. Dual citizenship grants all believers the authority to bring heaven here on earth. The yoke we wear with Christ does not just give us extra strength. Christ bestows us with authority, not to try and be little lords, but to extravagantly love the way He does. His authority allows us to drive away darkness that might hinder our brothers and sisters. His power enables us to sow hope, love, peace, and joy that supernaturally defeats despair, hate, fear, and depression.

When Jesus died, the veil to the Holy of Holies was torn from top to bottom, giving all believers access to His beautiful presence. No longer were only certain people granted access to the presence of God. We received access to heaven, became citizens of heaven, and because of this, we can be continuously filled with the Spirit that enables us to change the world.

When in Peru, I swam in the Amazon, explored ancient Inca ruins, and climbed Machu Picchu. I also successfully brought back from Peru about a dozen middle school and high school students without help from any of the other ministry leaders, and I'm proud to add that I did that without losing one of them! But none of those things come close to being as exciting or meaningful to me as the embrace from the woman in the market. When you partner with Christ, you take on an identity of lover, restorer, healer, and bringer of joy. You get to remind others of their immense value. You get to speak love that releases others from guilt, loneliness, and shame. You get to be there when others are reconciled back to the Heavenly Father that loves them. This is the adventure of being yoked with Christ and dual citizen of both heaven and earth. Nothing else can compare.

Reflections

1. Is there a particular people group or place or social problem that you desire to know more about? Are there social justice causes you want be a part of?

2. How might accepting your dual citizenship impact your involvement in such causes?

3. How can you act as an agent of peace, hope, joy and love in your everyday life?

Meditation

Read Matthew 11:28–30 several times. Ask Jesus to increase your awareness of His presence in your life and empower you in doing Kingdom work on earth.

NOTES

CHAPTER 3

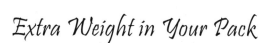

Extra Weight in Your Pack

In the film *Wild*, a young woman, Cheryl Strayed, embarks on a 1,100-mile hike of the Pacific Crest Trail. At one point in her journey, she makes a stop and receives some assistance from a more experienced hiker. He has her go through her enormous hiking pack, item by item, and asks her whether she really needs each thing. Essentially he helps Cheryl greatly lighten her pack. The extra weight was slowing her down, causing her unnecessary pain, and hindering the enjoyment of her hike. She eliminated the extra weight in her pack and set out for the rest of her journey with more enthusiasm, less pain, and the freedom to go at a faster pace.

Like Cheryl, we may need to lighten our load. When we set out from home for the first time, we often carry extra weight in our packs. The previous years may have taught us untruths about our loving God. We might have deep painful wounds from our childhood that have never healed. We might believe we are not worthy or capable of living a life that makes a difference.

You cannot fully accept a life of adventure with Christ, or the truth of your dual citizenship until you allow the Holy Spirit to help you clean out your pack. Holy Spirit wants to lead you into truth about who God is so that you can be healed and given a divine sense of purpose.

In college I had a hard time accepting forgiveness from Jesus. His grace seemed far removed, so partnership and authority with Him was not even on my radar. But He kept ushering me toward His love. I remember going to a chapel service in which the speaker talked about baggage and lined up several suitcases on the altar. She spoke about some of the sins or painful experiences that we let weigh us down. I started to feel overwhelmed. I thought maybe all of those suitcases belonged to me. I worried that everything wrong I had ever done was stacked up so high against me I might not ever be close to God.

Forgiveness releases complete freedom in Christ. And as soon as those thoughts entered my mind, the Holy Spirit reminded me that as far as the east is from the west that was how far removed my transgressions were from the mind of the Father. I think I actually felt grace for the first time in my life that night at chapel.

When Jesus was crucified a new era dawned on this world. Now there is no more need for animal sacrifices, no need for working to atone, no need for balancing scales, and certainly no need for guilt. Freedom in Christ means the forgiveness of sin—and much more. But you must truly accept forgiveness and know that God is not angry with you before experiencing the scope of the freedom found in Him. You have freedom to chase the dreams He placed deep within, even when they don't seem spiritual enough or they are scary or impractical. You have the freedom to reach out in friendship—with the love of Christ to those that might not have the best reputation, without worrying about raising eyebrows. You have the freedom to exercise authority over darkness and shine the light of Christ. This and more is what can take place when you accept the most beautiful part of faith. You are loved, and God will never use your shortcomings as ammo against you. He forgives, because His love for you is too great to let anything keep you at arm's length. He knows where you belong, and it's in His embrace.

Jesus is not content with mental assent to the concept of unconditional love. He won't let up until you feel it. Every day. Every moment. And it will become so compelling, so contagious that you won't let up until everyone knows the wonder of His love.

When a group of Pharisees bring a woman to Jesus they claim they caught in adultery, Jesus does not scold or lecture her about morality. He is not concerned with her feeling remorseful about any relations she might have had. He is concerned with her freedom, with saving her very life. He speaks to her accusers in such a way that they cannot help but relinquish their intent to harm her. Jesus frees her from blame. He protects her from harm. He gently points her toward the light after proving His love and care for her (see John 8: 3–11).

When Zacchaeus, a cheating tax collector, climbs into a tree to see Jesus, not only does Jesus not scold or lecture or condemn him, He invites Himself over for dinner! He creates an opportunity to be in community with Zacchaeus. This act of friendship is all it takes for Zacchaeus to repent of greed and receive a spirit of generosity to make restitution with even more than the amounts he cheated from people (see Luke 19: 2–10). Jesus set him free, giving him new life, new purpose, and a new hope for the future. Everyone else just judged him as a sinner, but Jesus was not out to judge him. He wanted to restore him. He did not incite feelings of remorse or guilt. Jesus healed Zacchaeus of shame. When Jesus loves you, you cannot keep from loving those around you with that kind of radical, transforming love.

When we grow in our relationship with Christ, when we receive deeper revelation of His character, love, and authority, we become more like Him. Learning to operate as Jesus would is one of the most powerful ways to bring heaven to earth. Without understanding and acceptance of Jesus' forgiveness, it is difficult to forgive others. When we don't believe He is crazy about us, we aren't crazy about others. It's unnatural to love people who are different from us. But when we believe He's not mad at us, we are secure in His love despite our shortcomings. His supernatural love flows through us and transforms all of our relationships. We can forgive and restore, even when we've been truly hurt. We can build relationships with those the religious crowd condemns. We can invite others to a place of rest, love, kindness and justice. Jesus came to invite everyone into a beautiful, close adventurous relationship with him. When we partner with Him, we get to help everyone we meet experience the transformative relationship we've experienced.

Some of us leave home for the first time with deep emotional wounds. We might have experienced loss, abuse, rejection, or neglect from those who were supposed to love us the most. The good news is that our loving God is ready and able to take us through a healing process. He does not want that pain to hurt us forever. He wants to bring complete healing and restoration to our physical, emotional, and spiritual selves.

In my years working in higher education I have counseled students going through the emotional pain of their parents' divorce, a tough break-up, verbal abuse from parents, the trauma associated with date rape and sexual assault, and many other situations. And though pastoral counseling and encouragement has been helpful to them, many, many times the Holy Spirit also uses professional counselors and psychologists to help them come to a place of complete healing.

The Holy Spirit is more than able to instantaneously correct an untruthful thought or provide comfort to someone in pain. But He also created people with a special gift for helping people through the healing process. And He loves empowering His children to help His other children! If you are dealing with a painful past or a traumatic occurrence, seek out the help of a pastoral counselor, campus counselor, or professional counselor in the community. If you are not sure who to talk to, ask a trusted friend. Chances are you have a number of friends who have also received help from a counseling professional.

But you don't have to have gone through serious trauma or emotional pain to doubt your potential to impact your community and world for the Kingdom. Sometimes very subtle messages reinforce the lie that you are not qualified for the work God has placed in your heart. Accepting new truth often helps defeat the untruths we've allowed in our hearts and minds. Reading books, blogs, sermons, and songs by brothers and sisters like Graham Cooke, Bill Johnson, Mimi Haddad, David Benner, Kim Walker, and many others have personally helped me.

The practice of *soaking*, spending significant time resting in the presence of God, has also become a transformative practice in my own life. Taking time in the day to simply lay down and ask Holy Spirit to fill you with rest, peace, and love is a powerful way to let our loving God affirm the truth about His nature. In those moments you will feel His love in such a tangible way, as well as receive new revelation about who you are in Him. Adventure is not all about movement or business. The rest is just as essential to the journey as activity.

Just as her fellow hiker liberated Cheryl Strayed from the extra weight in her pack, the Holy Spirit will liberate us from anything weighing us down. His life-giving truth will undo the damage of the lies we've believed. His overwhelming love heals our hurts. His deep, peaceful rest reminds us of our immense value to Him. He cares for us so much. We need only to pause long enough for Him to remind us of this.

Reflections

1. Do you struggle to believe God is not mad at you? What ideas do you need to unload out of your pack?

2. Would you benefit from seeing a counselor about some of the past hurts or trauma? Who could you seek out for that kind of help?

3. Do you doubt your God-given strengths and abilities? How could you gain more confidence in your value to the Kingdom?

Meditation

Ask your Heavenly Father to show you the depths of His love for you. Ask Jesus to convince you of His complete forgiveness and grace. Ask Holy Spirit to help you see yourself the way He does.

NOTES

ADVENTURE AVAILABLE

CHAPTER 4

❖

Choosing A Path

Y ou do not just end up somewhere. You make turns, choose side streets, accelerate or stop. When you reach your destination, you've made a multitude of decisions as you traveled. I did not just end up in my current life situation. I established a pattern of living with Jesus, partnered with Him in the most important decisions of my life. I'm experiencing the tangible, exciting reality of what it means to say "yes" to the invitation, "Come follow me."

When I said "yes" to Jesus in that one-woman tent in the mountains of West Virginia, I had hardly had any idea about the things that lay in store for me in the most important decade of my life. And if you told me one of the first things this partnership would mean would be to give up my almost life-long dream of working in politics, I would have laughed at you.

My whole life people told me I would make a great ambassador, senator, or lawyer. I almost did not go to Emmanuel College because they had no political science program and I did not want to limit my career by choosing something as narrow as pre-law. But the Holy Spirit began prompting my heart about studying ministry. I realized that I enjoyed my Bible class more than my first law classes, but I could not let go of that part of my identity yet.

After another semester, I continued to feel the prompting, but my reluctance had a new reason to grow. Even though at that point I actually wanted to change my major to ministry, even though I was taking all the extra Bible classes I could cram into my schedule, I faced a huge obstacle. I started dating my good friend Rick at the beginning of my sophomore year and he was a ministry major. I just could not be that girl who switched to the major of her boyfriend! I could not stand the thought of my peers speculating that I gave up my promising political career so that I could play the organ and teach Sunday school at the church my husband pastored. It made me sick to my stomach.

Jesus had to convince me. I told Him that I just could not stand the potential gossip and judgment, and that I could glean all I needed from just minoring in ministry. But I could not even convince myself. He spoke clearly to my spirit in a moment of prayer "You'll be fine either way. Really. But if you want what will be most fulfilling, trust Me on this one."

And I did, because pride and fear really don't seem such great decision making tools compared to knowing the Creator is ushering you into His best for your life.

When God worked to knit you together in your mother's womb, He hoped. He hoped you would say "yes" to His promptings. He hoped you would listen, not because He is super controlling, but because He knows you intimately. He knows your thoughts, your feelings, your deepest desires and fears. God knows what will satisfy your soul because He designed you. When He invites you to do something that seems strange or impractical or scary, say "yes." It will be the first step into the greatest adventure of your life.

Changing your initial career plan can be scary. When mom or dad or other friends and family express disapproval, the Holy Spirit will comfort and affirm you. When you doubt your own ability, Jesus will stand side by side with you. When obstacles come your way, our Heavenly Father will protect and defend you. Often God will put other people in your life to confirm His calling. An administrator working in the career center, your academic advisor, a pastor or mentor, or friend might also confirm that they too see the gifts our Creator put in you. And if you are not getting any input from these types of people, seek them out! If you are in the college context, there is most likely a team of wonderful people waiting to invest in your future. You just need to take the first step and ask for help. If you are not in college, consult mentors, pastors, and colleagues that you trust.

I've seen students blow it big time. Seriously blow it. I've witnessed capable, smart individuals waste twenty thousand dollars in tuition money to sit in their dorm rooms and play Halo rather than study and skateboard around campus in the middle of day rather than go to their classes. If I were going to blow twenty stacks, I would find out when the next U2 tour is and chase them around Europe listen to fantastic rock, explore the Irish countryside, and eat and drink at the finest pubs.

There is no way I would pay twenty thousand dollars to sit in a cramped dorm room just to live off a diet of Ramen noodles, Hot Pockets, and Mountain Dew and have nothing to show for it but a 0.0 GPA.

But students all over the country do this. Every semester students fail, drop out, and give up. This does not happen because they did not learn how to study in high school or because their brains have not fully matured or because their parents never imparted to them a decent work ethic, even though those things might be true of any given student. This happens because they are making decisions without the revelation that their Creator has a great, meaningful, calling on their life. They know they probably need an education so they can get a job to have money for food, clothing, and shelter, but without an understanding of vocation, there is no drive to make the choices that lead to graduation day, a successful career, and all that could come afterward.

Words like *calling* and *vocation* used to scare me. Repulsed by the thought of the divine mapping out my future step-by-step, I dismissed vocation because I thought that meant limits and surrendering my real desires. I also did not know my Maker the way I do now. I did not know then that "it is for freedom that Christ has set us free" (Galatians 5:1). I did not know then that my Heavenly Father knows me so well, that He could only ever usher me into deeper intimacy and adventure with Him. I did not know then that rather than urging me down a predetermined road map, Holy Spirit prompts us with daily questions like, "Where do you want to go? Whom do you want to love generously? What do you want to dream with Me about?" Now vocation and calling seem liberating, not constricting. Now I know it does not mean forfeiting my real purpose; it means driving head first into the most satisfying, craziest fulfilling life I could ever hope for.

Saying God has a plan for your life may sound trite, like an old tract or fortune cookie. But knowing your Creator, the depths at which He knows you, and experiencing what life looks like when you do it together is beautiful. Beauty does not come easily. There is hard work. There is sacrifice. There is saying no to that party and choosing to stop playing Halo before midnight instead of 4 AM. There is lots and lots and lots of time spent studying in the library. But there is also the satisfaction of cultivating discipline in your life. There are restful nights filled with adequate sleep, enjoying your classes, and success.

I love the passage in the Bible when Jesus calls Peter, Andrew, James, and John to leave their fishing nets and become fishers of men with Him.

> *As Jesus was walking beside the Sea of Galilee, he saw two brothers, Simon called Peter and his brother Andrew. They were casting a net into the lake, for they were fishermen. "Come, follow me," Jesus said, "and I will send you out to fish for people." At once they left their nets and followed Him. Going on from there, he saw two other brothers, James son of Zebedee and his brother John. They were in a boat with their father Zebedee, preparing their nets. Jesus called them, and immediately they left the boat and their father and followed Him.*

—MATTHEW 4:18–22

Notice that they do not even hesitate. Not one of them even asks Him for more clarity about what fishing for men might entail. They immediately drop what they are doing and follow Him. Why is that I wonder? Could they all have hated fishing that much? I'm quite sure it had more to do with the attractiveness of Jesus's love and purpose. It is unlikely that they would have been contemplating a new profession. They fished because that is what they knew, that is what their fathers did, and that is how they ate, traded, and survived. But Jesus drew them to Himself. He knew them, and they knew immediately that they wanted to know Him too. Vocation is not really about making a living. Calling is about Who is calling you. You don't need all the details about your life's story to move forward and make decisions. You just need to know Who you are following.

Peter and Andrew lived partnered with Christ, long after He ascended back into Heaven. They did not just find Jesus an attractive leader or a thoughtful teacher or revolutionary advocate for social justice. They knew His love and deeply loved Him in return. History tells us that these two preached the Gospel all across the world. They proclaimed the news of our Heavenly Father's goodness, just as they had seen Jesus do. They also died the way Jesus died. Hung on a scandalous cross, they gave up their very breath for the One that radically touched their lives with love, truth, and freedom.

I think a lot of students are under the misconception that if you decide to partner with Christ, He will only make you either a missionary or an evangelist. This is true in a way—when you partner with Christ your entire purpose becomes about bringing the good news to all you meet. You love advancing the mission to reconcile all things back to a heavenly state. But this does not mean you can only work in a church vocation. Our God loves variety, and there is a great variety in the ways we will be called to serve Him.

The good news comes in all kinds of forms. Art, music, dance, film, and writing become avenues to bring Kingdom here on earth. Professionals like fire fighters, graphic designers, teachers, counselors, government officials, accountants, and engineers get unique opportunities to share light and love. The avenues to communicate Christ's compassion and grace are endless. There's no way you'll get stuck doing something you hate when you partner with Christ because He wants you to experience full, abundant life.

I know a lot of students who resist life in community with our loving God because they do not want to give up their hopes, plans, and dreams for their lives. What many of them fail to realize is that so often those hopes, plans, and dreams were placed in their heart by their Creator. He is not interested in them abandoning those things to live a life of misery. He simply asks that we first follow Him in faith. Then we see how He causes those exciting hope, plans, and dreams to become reality.

When you seek first the King and His Kingdom you don't have to worry about your needs being met. This is the promise of provision seen in Matthew 6:25–34. You also can rest in the fact that God does not stop with providing your basic physical needs. God also loves to give us all kinds of good gifts.

Ask and it will be given to you; seek and you will find; knock and the door will be opened to you. For everyone who asks receives; the one who seeks finds; and to the one who knocks, the door will be opened. Which of you, if your son asks for bread, will give him a stone? Or if he asks for a fish, will give him a snake? If you, then, though you are evil, know how to give good gifts to your children, how much more will your Father in heaven give good gifts to those who ask him! So in everything, do to others what you would have them do to you, for this sums up the Law and the Prophets.

—MATTHEW 7:7–12

It does not matter if you go to technical college, study graphic design, attend the best medical school to attempt to find a cure for cancer, or pick a trade that does not require a college degree. What matters is that you enter into relationship with the One who knows your deepest desires, your giftings, and what gives you deep and lasting satisfaction. God has a plan for you, and that plan is for you to follow Him—to live life with Him. The rest is not just minor details. The rest is stepping into a journey filled with happiness, sacrifice, perseverance, hope, and meaning. The rest is receiving the beautiful gifts He wants to lavish over us and returning that love and grace to those around us. Creating with your Creator is the real meaning of calling.

Reflections

1. What do you typically associate with the terms vocation or calling?

2. Do you have a clear sense of your life calling or a career you want to pursue? If yes, what is it? If not, who could you consult with to help discover that calling?

3. What would you like to be doing five years after graduation? What choices are you making today that are preparing you for those goals?

Meditation

Think about some of your career goals and ask your Heavenly Father to show you opportunities within those fields to sow heaven on earth.

NOTES

ADVENTURE AVAILABLE

CHAPTER 5

Using Dynamite and Other Explosives

When I was in Peru I had this idea about how to make every week in college like a mission trip. I started making a list of people in need within driving distance from my college campus.

1. Nursing home residents

2. Housing authority after school participants

3. Domestic violence shelter residents

4. Food pantry recipients

5. Homeless residents at local shelter

6. Actual homeless people in Atlanta

And then I started thinking of ways my peers and I could love them.

1. Sing carols and make Christmas cards for the elderly.

2. Start mentorship program for kids.

3. Distribute care packages for displaced moms and kids

4. Donate and serve food.

5. Collect and distribute blankets.

6. Pack sack lunches and feed the homeless.

None of the student programs through the college I attended were doing any of these activities. The opportunity to plan and implement such service opportunities was before me and I really had only two options. I could wait for a school administrator to start something like this and hop in, or I could recruit help and start something new. The first option seemed boring and unrealistic. What are the chances of someone else just dreaming this up too?

So I went with option two. I solicited help from some wonderful people. Our campus pastor, Chris, appreciated my idea so much he let me have an entire chapel service to talk about Matthew 25 and some problems in our little corner of the world and how we as Christ-partners could be solutions to some of these problems. The Service Learning Coordinator, Regina, took me under her wing and really invested a lot of her time in me. She encouraged my passion, while making sure to ask enough questions to get me thinking critically about logistics and the long-term impact.

So many of my peers stepped up to help, it was like an army rose up on campus. With just a chapel service and some sign-up sheets and a few fliers, our movement mobilized students all over the community. We sold concessions for hours at football games to raise money for the local crisis pregnancy center. We collected blankets and walked around downtown Athens giving them out to any cold homeless man or woman. We made care packages for the local domestic violence shelter. We collected socks and underwear for the children that lived in government housing complexes. We sang carols and hymns at the nursing home.

Some of the projects evolved in ways I could never have imagined. After talking to some of the staff at the homeless shelter we learned a lot of the residents received disability or social security checks, but it was not uncommon for them to spend all the money on one or two nights in a nice hotel and then live unprotected the other twenty-eight days of the month. My friend Lauren decided to get several business majors together and host workshops at the shelter on how to budget those checks in a way that could last all month.

We also learned from the director of the women's shelter that though they received toiletries often, there was always a shortage of black hair products. We were able to stock up their supplies with shampoo, conditioner, and other products for black hair.

By far my favorite thing we did through this initiative was a program called Peanut Butter and Jesus. A team of eight to twelve students would meet in the cafeteria and make about fifty sack lunches with little notes about how Jesus cares about their salvation and He also deeply cares about their physical and emotional well-being. We drove to Atlanta about once a month to hand out the lunches, talk, and pray with the homeless people we would meet.

Twenty-somethings are powerful, and their potential is unquantifiable. They have a real thirst to make a difference in the world. They are full of energy, creativity, and the courage to start something new without anyone else begging and pleading with them. They thirst for justice, not just in their own corner of the world but across the globe. They actually believe they can end modern day slavery, the global oppression and abuse of women, the clean water crisis, institutional racism, and poverty. They have hope. And when twenty-somethings partner with Christ they do not just have naïve hope, they have a hope that anchors their souls.

Jesus taught his disciples to pray for things radical and things practical. He gave them this short prayer that we still pray today.

> *Our Father in heaven,*
> *Hallowed be your name,*
> *Your kingdom come,*
> *Your will be done,*
> *On earth as it is in heaven.*
> *Give us today our daily bread.*
> *And forgive us our debts,*
> *As we also have forgiven our debtors.*

And do not lead us not into temptation,
But deliver us from the evil one.

For Yours is the kingdom and the power and the glory
forever. Amen.

—MATTHEW 6: 9–13

Your Kingdom come, your will be done, on earth as it is in heaven. *On earth as it is in heaven!* Again, we are reminded of our dual citizenship and our authority to see our world look more like heaven. In your prayers, what places on the earth do you want to invade with heaven? In your life, how are you bringing the things of heaven into earthly situations? Do you want to adopt orphans? Do you want to prosecute perpetuators of injustice? Do you want to build wells where there is no clean drinking water? Do you want to feed the hungry? Do you want to provide for expectant mothers in crisis? Do you want to look after children with neglectful parents? Do you want to protect women and children from sexual predators? Do you want to break the cycle of systematic racism? Do you want to lay hands on the sick and see them made well? Do you want to comfort those dying of the AIDS virus?

When we pray, "on earth as it is in heaven" and are partnered with Christ, we cannot tolerate certain things anymore. We cannot show indifference towards the suffering of others. We cannot sit passively when we know we carry the presence of the living God. We have the Holy Spirit inside of us. We contend for things like peace, justice, mercy, blessing, and unconditional love. We serve as agents of reconciliation.

When we are not sure what course of action to take in a situation—we look to our Savior. Jesus modeled for us what it means to bring heaven to earth. When He saw those with sickness He brought healing. Where He saw those in isolation, He brought them into community. When He saw those in danger, He protected them. When He saw those with corruption in their lives, He offered redemption. When He saw the oppressive, self-righteous religious, He rebuked them. When He saw children, He welcomed them. When He interacted with women, He restored the dignity society had taken from them. When He saw his friends mourn, He cried with them.

Jesus brought heaven to earth. And when we serve as His ambassadors, He gives us the same opportunity. We all have a unique calling, but we share in the same purpose. This describes our work with Christ:

> *Since, then, we know what it is to fear the Lord, we try to persuade others. What we are is plain to God, and I hope it is also plain to your conscience. We are not trying to commend ourselves to you again, but are giving you an opportunity to take pride in us, so that you can answer those who take pride in what is seen rather than in what is in the heart. If we are "out of our mind," as some say, it is for God; if we are in our right mind, it is for you. For Christ's love compels us, because we are convinced that one died for all, and therefore all died. And he died for all, that those who live should no longer live for themselves but for him who died for them and was raised again.*
>
> *So from now on we regard no one from a worldly point of view. Though we once regarded Christ in this way, we do so no*

longer. Therefore, if anyone is in Christ, the new creation has come: The old has gone, the new is here! All this is from God, who reconciled us to himself through Christ and gave us the ministry of reconciliation: that God was reconciling the world to himself in Christ, not counting people's sins against them. And he has committed to us the message of reconciliation. We are therefore Christ's ambassadors, as though God were making his appeal through us. We implore you on Christ's behalf: Be reconciled to God. God made him who had no sin to be sin for us, so that in him we might become the righteousness of God.

—2 CORINTHIANS 5:11–21

We are Christ's ambassadors, as though God were making his appeal through us (see 2 Corinthians 5:20). Our very lives should remind everyone we meet that God is good, that He redeems, that He makes all things new. When partnered with Christ, our lives demonstrate His love, compassion, grace, protection, and justice. This is why we are partnered with Christ. We cannot represent Him, without Him working through us.

I traveled to Nashville to work with a church that actively served the local homeless population. They took us to a café that had its own garden where they served homeless individuals free meals that they made from this garden and other donated supplies. One of the guys who worked there shared that some people trying to feed the hungry were actually just helping the homeless die faster. I thought this was pretty jarring, but he continued. He told us most homeless people suffer from diabetes and that the most common food available at any given food panty or shelter is pastry, loaded with sugar. Rather than allowing people to die from hunger many were killing them slowly with cream cheese frosting.

Helping can actually hurt people when it is done the wrong way. I walked away from that experience with the unsettling feeling that maybe some of my own attempts to help the hurting were not well thought out. The truth is that sometimes what we can do quickly and easily actually does more harm than good. Sustainable social change takes both compassion and deep understanding of the problem. Compassion must be accompanied by research, communication, common sense and perseverance. I could not let that sobering reality stop me from trying to help, but I knew some things needed to change.

One of the first adjustments I made to some of the service projects I led was the menu. We used to grill hot dogs and give out chips and fruit punch to the children we mentored with the local housing authority. We changed things up and started grilling chicken for subs on whole wheat bread and served carrots and raisins as the sides with water or juice with no sugar added. We also got some of the exercise science majors to come talk to the kids about how to eat healthy in a school cafeteria. Some of the athletes on campus started hosting clinics after school to promote exercise and athletic activity. Obesity and diabetes are not at all uncommon among low-income children, and I resolved to help break this cycle. These efforts required more manpower and more money. But I was not interested in us simply easing our conscience and patting ourselves on the back for spending time with these children. When you care about those you serve, the extra time, energy, and money are worth the lasting change you ultimately can have on the overall quality of their lives.

When you partner with Christ, He will give you His passion to serve the poor, the brokenhearted, and the marginalized. You might feel compelled to address a certain social problem. Or maybe you haven't found your niche yet. Maybe you've been on the lookout for ways to address these issues on your campus or in your community but can't seem to find the right organization or campus group to join. I think a lot of times in life you are not going to stumble upon an easy avenue to do some of the things God has placed in your heart. I think sometimes rather than finding your niche you have to get out a stick of dynamite and create your niche! Just make sure before you use those explosives that you consult a demolition expert. God fills our hearts with compassion and equips us with wisdom.

Twenty-somethings are some of the freest individuals in society. Freedom in mobility, in relationships, and in dreaming for the future all characterize this part of your life journey. But don't just dream. Don't wait until you're a PhD or a millionaire to start changing the world. Empowered by the Holy Spirit you can use your twenties to bring God's Kingdom here on earth, just as it is in heaven.

Reflection

1. Do you desire to start a new ministry or outreach in your community? What is it?

2. What experts could you consult before getting started? What steps can you take to make sure your efforts to help don't hurt over time?

3. Do you have other friends who share your passion? How might you encourage them to partner with you?

Meditation

Ask our Heavenly Father to break your heart for the things that break His heart, and allow the Holy Spirit to fill you with wisdom regarding how you should get involved.

NOTES

CHAPTER 6

Companions for the Journey

I thought my first roommate in college was a little weird. Before I met her face to face, we set up a phone date to work out the logistics of who would bring the microwave and who would bring the mini-fridge and other details like that. During our first phone conversation I learned some details about my soon-to-be roommate, Joy, that made me nervous. She told me she did not listen to any non-Christian music. A big alarm bell went off in my head. She also wanted to pray for me at the end of the conversation. Another alarm bell went off. Don't get me wrong. I loved Jesus, but this girl struck me as odd—certainly more restrictive than necessary. I started having nightmares that she was going to burn all my Radiohead and U2 albums and get me to wear a WWJD bracelet while chanting some tune by Sandi Patti. You should have seen her face when she came into our room for the first time. I already had my *Harry Potter and the Prisoner of Azkaban* movie poster on the wall and I think maybe she might have contemplated exorcising our cramped space.

I figured Joy and I were never going to be friends so we did not really hang out much outside or inside of our room. I stuck with my male rafting buddies and a few other girls I had gotten to know and grew very comfortable in my cozy little social circle. Even when I needed to do homework or study, I went to a basement lobby, listened to *The Bends* album by Radiohead on repeat, and highlighted in my text books.

Not too long after the start of my first semester, I got sick. And Joy did something that surprised me—she took care of me. She followed me to the bathroom with my toothbrush and laid it out with toothpaste already on it when I had to puke, just so I could freshen up right afterwards. She made me a bed on the floor so I would not have to leap from my top bunk every time I had to run to the toilet. She prayed for me to feel well again. This was the same girl I thought was too much of a Jesus nerd to be friends with, but she taught me that you can be friends with people who don't think exactly like you.

Friendship is one of the best parts about your twenties. You might have, or have had, great friends from high school, but usually you remain close to only a handful of them. College and early adulthood is a great time to make meaningful connections with people who are both likeminded and very different from you.

Close friendships take time. You actually have to spend time getting to know people before you really know them. The sad thing is that some college students quit on college because they don't make friends instantly. One year when I was a college administrator, I was approached by three freshmen asking to withdrawal from school before classes had even begun. They all stated basically the same reason: they were homesick, not ready for dorm life, and felt everyone—except them—already knew everyone else. Despite my explaining to them that even though they felt lonely, and it appeared that lots of people already knew each other, they were not the only ones who were feeling this way and they would soon make some awesome friends if they just gave it a semester, a month, at least a week!

Sadly, friendship for some students has become more awkward and more self-focused. Everyone can text, but not many can just approach people and initiate a conversation. Everyone can join a group on Facebook, but not everyone will join a new club or student organization. Some will communicate their most intimate feelings in a Tweet, but few have someone they talk to about the deepest places of their hearts and minds.

The good news is that for those who follow Christ we have a savior who is always ready and waiting to teach us how to be good friends. Our culture does not have to doom us to superficial friendships or hinder our ability to be a good friend to others. Despite the rise of social technology and our dependence on it, Jesus will help us to be great friends, face to face, in living color.

Learning to be a good friend is one of the most important skills to master throughout your life, and college and early adulthood is a phenomenal place to begin practicing the art of friendship. Though you might not take any academic courses on the subject of close relationships, you'll have plenty of opportunity to navigate a variety of situations that will help you develop the skill needed to be a great, life-long friend.

Clueless about the makings of a good friend? Here are some helpful tips:

- Friendship takes time. Don't be frustrated if you're not close after one month of hanging out with someone. Closeness is developed through a process.

- Good friends show kindness, even in the face of unkindness.

- Friends don't get jealous when their friends succeed. They rejoice in the victories of the ones they love.

- Friends don't think they are too good for their friends. They prefer their friend's wants and needs above their own.

- Friends make time for one another. They honor one another by investing time and energy to encourage, value, and respect their loved ones.

- Friends don't get mad easily. They take time to understand any situation and exercise grace when they've been wronged or hurt. And they definitely don't hold grudges when wrong has been done because forgiveness covers any pain caused.

- Friends call their friends into deeper knowledge of their strengths, gifts, and talents. A friend affirms the things God has placed inside you.

- Friends don't give up on those they love.

Does this sound familiar? I know this verse is read at many weddings, but it is the most comprehensive, powerful description of what friendship looks like in the Kingdom of God.

Love is patient, love is kind. It does not envy, it does not boast, it is not proud. It does not dishonor others, it is not self-seeking, it is not easily angered, it keeps no record of wrongs. Love does not delight in evil but rejoices with the truth. It always protects, always trusts, always hopes, always perseveres. Love never fails.

—1 CORINTHIANS 13: 4–8a

Let's look at a story that shows Jesus restoring Peter.

When they had finished eating, Jesus said to Simon Peter, "Simon son of John, do you love me more than these?"

"Yes, Lord," he said, "you know that I love you."

Jesus said, "Feed my lambs."

Again Jesus said, "Simon son of John, do you love me?"

He answered, "Yes, Lord, you know that I love you."

Jesus said, "Take care of my sheep."

The third time He said to him, "Simon son of John, do you love me?"

Peter was hurt because Jesus asked him the third time, "Do you love me?" He said, "Lord, you know all things; you know that I love you."

Jesus said, "Feed my sheep.

—JOHN 21: 15–17

Peter had denied he ever knew Jesus—renounced Him. Peter did not stick with Jesus through the crucifixion like John did, because he was too scared. Jesus gives Peter three opportunities to tell him how he loves him, because that is how many times he denied Jesus. Jesus, rather than scolding him for his friendship failure, helps Peter heal. And not only that, but Jesus tells Peter who he really is. He gives him these simple commands like "Feed my sheep, feed my lambs, and take care of my sheep." Jesus reaffirms Peter's call to pastor—three times—and lets him know that despite his denial, Peter is a shepherd who will care for others and lead them into transforming truth.

When was the last time a friend failed you? Did you just sweep it under the rug because you did not want to have the tough conversation? Did you get mad and dismiss your friend, justifying yourself by claiming you deserved better? Did you recognize the deeper reality, that even though they might have failed, their failure is not their defining characteristic? Did you affirm the gifts in them?

I know we are supposed to give recognition to the gifts in our friends because this is what Jesus does for us. I dealt with a lot of insecurities in college, but you never would have guessed it. I was always very confident in my activities. I never doubted I could lead an organization well, start a successful campus ministry, or get good grades. I knew I was assertive, creative, and intelligent when it came time for action. But I had all these false ideas about myself, that I was nothing without my titles, insignificant without my responsibilities.

I knew some of the thoughts I had about myself were not coming from my Heavenly Father and I wanted to deal with that. I wanted to like myself, without having to do anything. One night Jesus helped me make a list of things that I thought about myself that I knew were not really true. After I finished writing out all the lies I believed about myself, I rejected this false self I had created and then I burned my list. Talk about liberation! Holy Spirit started healing some really tender parts of my heart. Then I felt prompted to make a new list. I let the Holy Spirit speak truth over me. I made a new list, and I still have that list today.

When you partner with Jesus in this life, He is an awesome friend to you. He calls out the best in you, especially in times when you've just fallen flat on your face. And He encourages us to do the same. He wants us to see the truth about our friends, the good, beautiful truth He placed inside them. Our friends fail, just like we do. They offend, they disappoint, and they hurt us. This is the nature of intimate relationships. Even though close relationships bring so much joy, there is going to be pain involved too. But the hurts are just an opportunity to grow closer together and grow more into the image of Jesus.

In my freshman year of college, I found out one of my best friends was habitually lying to me and the rest of her close friends. Sometimes it would be about something trivial like a story about getting a speeding ticket. Other times her tales would be very elaborate like a close friend from home committing suicide. There really was not any story or situation she was not willing to conjure up to manipulate her friends around her.

After catching her in one of her biggest lies, I decided I had to do something. I could not let her continue this unhealthy, damaging pattern she had established. I convinced two other friends who loved her as much as I did to basically have an intervention for her, off-campus, where we could just be alone together and help her work out this junk. I told her I was angry with her and expressed how hurt I was by her willingness to destroy our trust for extra attention. But then I told her I still loved her and would not give up on her. Her other two friends conveyed the same sentiment.

I would love to tell you she never lied again and that we remain close friends today, but that's not the case. We still hung out occasionally but she migrated to a new social crew and eventually dropped out of school. Several years later I met up with her for dinner to catch up. Over our bowls of noodles, she began describing another new group of friends and then made a comment that caught me completely off guard. She said, "I like my friends, but they are not close like we are." Close like we are? We had not even spoken in person for at least a year.

This friend's parents divorced when she was really young. She learned as a little girl if you wanted to be cared for, if you wanted to be loved, something had to be going wrong in your life. She learned people don't show concern unless you give them a really big, dramatic reason. And perhaps the three of us that night, in our ever so awkward but necessary intervention, communicated to her for the first time not only would we love her without the fantastic stories, but we'd forgive all the hurts and lies because she was still worth loving.

Someone who lies is not a liar. Sure my friend lied. She lied a lot. But to just sum up her complex being by saying, "That girl is a liar," would be completely unfair. Sometimes when people offend us, we want to sum up their total being by their one mistake, or their many, many mistakes. But this completely disrespects that fact that they were carefully and wonderfully made by a loving God who is crazy about them.

I wanted to sum up Joy as a religious nut just because she exclusively listened to Christian music. A lot of my peers summed up my other friend as a liar and a manipulator. I can't help but wonder how many people miss out on close friendships because they make quick judgments and assumptions that reduce people to one quirk or one fault.

Perhaps you struggle with believing God is loving and gracious and forgives all your sins because you haven't experienced this with close personal relationships here on earth. Perhaps your friends do too. But what if we changed this? What if we did love of our friends in the midst of their struggles? What if we never reduced their personhood to that one thing that rubbed us the wrong way or hurt us? What if we could appreciate the people in our life with totally opposite personalities, viewpoints, and interests? How much easier might it be to accept the love and forgiveness of our Heavenly Father if we experienced a similar grace from our friends when we failed?

Friendship is not just an important skill to master in your life. Friendship is one of the most powerful tools Christ gives us to build the kingdom of God on earth, just as it is in heaven. Through our friendships we learn trust and grace and brotherly and sisterly love. Through our friendships we are blessed with joy, companionship, fun, and support. Through close friendships we have the opportunity to call out all the heaven we see in our loved ones. We get to usher our loved ones into deeper revelation of our loving God. We receive deeper revelation of our relationship-centered God. Are there heartaches involved? Sure thing. But nothing compares to the joys of close friendships. They are a beautiful glimpse of heaven here on earth.

Reflections

1. Is there a friend in your life who needs your forgiveness? How can you help restore your relationship?

2. What are some practical ways you can grow in your ability to befriend others?

3. How can you help some of your friends see more clearly their value to God?

Meditation

Pick a friend who needs encouragement and ask Holy Spirit for divine revelation about their purpose and value.

NOTES

_____

_____

_____

_____

_____

_____

_____

_____

_____

_____

_____

_____

_____

_____

_____

_____

_____

_____

ADVENTURE AVAILABLE

CHAPTER 7

Two Warriors

During my first week of college, when I was in line in the cafeteria, this guy came up to me and asked my name. When I told him that my name was Margaret, he asked if he could call me Maggie. I thought that was pretty presumptuous of him. But I did not know him from the other eight hundred new peers so I shrugged it off and said, "Sure, Dude. Call me Maggie." I thought I'd probably not even run into him again.

But I did. A few months later he asked me to go rafting in West Virginia. This guy was quickly becoming my closest friend. A few weeks after our return from the Gauley River rafting experience, he asked if we could start praying together once a week, and we did. We jogged together, we studied together, and we confided in one another. When I went home for Thanksgiving break we talked on the phone every day.

Right before Christmas break we went to a concert on campus. At this point Rick had absolutely become my best friend. I knew he loved and cared for me. I knew I loved and cared for him. Time was better when we were together. Rick, jamming about in the mosh pit, chipped his front tooth on the stage. It was in that moment that the Holy Spirit spoke something beautiful yet scary to my spirit, "You two are going to suffer for the Gospel together." My love for Rick grew immensely in that moment, as I considered being partnered together with him in this adventurous life with Christ. All of a sudden, looking into those blue eyes and at that smile with almost an entire front tooth missing I thought, *I want to spend the rest of my life with Rick Turner.* As I write this, we've been married for seven years—and I'm loving it!

When we got engaged I remember browsing through the marriage section at a Christian bookstore and being repulsed by some of the content I discovered. I saw lots of strange messages in these books like, women need love (men don't?), but men need respect (women don't?), or men should be the providers while a wife's ultimate destiny is to be beautiful and adoring of her strong husband. But possibly the most disturbing message I picked up on is that so many of these authors were describing marriage as a battle with one's partner. Some went so far as to say that in the end, it was a drudgingly difficult task to choose to love one's partner when feelings of romance and affection had ceased. *That's a load of crap* I thought.

After seven years of marriage I'm still convinced that all of that is a load of crap. For Rick and I, our relationship has been a tremendous blessing, and it has also been really fun. Do we fight? We sure do. But our conflicts are typically resolved quickly because we both seek to love and honor the other. I don't dutifully choose to love Rick. I'm still crazy about him. I am still in awe of the fact that God blessed us with each other's love and empowerment.

I think there are a lot of couples that miss out on God's best for their marriages because they don't understand God's ultimate purpose for marriage. In Scripture we see something amazing.

> *Then God said, "Let us make mankind in our image, in our likeness, so that they may rule over the fish in the sea and the birds in the sky, over the livestock and all the wild animals, and over all the creatures that move along the ground."*
>
> *So God created mankind in his own image, in the image of God he created them; male and female he created them.*
>
> *God blessed them and said to them, "Be fruitful and increase in number; fill the earth and subdue it. Rule over the fish in the sea and the birds in the sky and over every living creature that moves on the ground."*
>
> —GENESIS 1:26–28

Our Triune God, one God in three persons—Father, Son and Holy Spirit—created man and woman in Their image. The fact that God is a Trinity means there has been community for all eternity. When we look at the Trinity we see that there is both commonality and uniqueness, and constant fellowship with mutual love, mutual submission and mutual empowerment. This is God's desire for all of us when God said "Let's make mankind in our image." All three members were active participants in weaving together everything that makes us unique beings. Thus, since the marriage relationship is the closest earthly relationship we have, there should be a special priority to loving one another, submitting to one another, and empowering one another. That is how real intimacy is cultivated.

Notice that God tells *them* to rule over the creatures of the earth together, but not to rule over each other. *After* the fall God describes a world where the husband rules over the wife— but it is part of the curse—it is descriptive not prescriptive!

My sister had the brilliant idea of making a t-shirt that read, "Egalitarians have better sex." In my own life and in counseling other women, I have found this to be so true! Couples who advocate for each other, lead their families together, encourage the use of the gifts God has given the other, experience the gift of spiritual, emotional, and sexual intimacy. Whereas couples who pin all responsibility on one or the other, who limit each other or try to change each other, miss out on the beautifully deep closeness that could be otherwise available to them.

There is a very key element for our marriages that sometimes we miss out on when we just glance over certain passages and take them for face value without digging deeper. In Genesis we come across this verse:

> *The Lord God said, "It is not good for the man to be alone. I will make a helper suitable for him."*

> —Genesis 2:18

This passage used to rub me the wrong way. I thought "helper" meant God wanted Adam to have a lady friend around to pack him sack lunches and fold his laundry. But this is very far from the intent. The Hebrew word for "helper" is *ezer* and is most commonly used to describe God coming to the rescue of His people. It is also commonly used to describe a warrior coming to the rescue of his people in a battle. God is not saying He made Adam a domestic aid. He is saying He is creating a fellow warrior.

So we have two very prominent ideas laid at the earth's creation before sin ever entered into the picture. The first is that man and woman were created in the image of the Triune God and have been given the power to rule over the earth together. The second is that men and women were created as fellow warriors.

These two ideas guide Rick and me in our marriage. We lead together or co-lead in our family, our church, and our greater community. We see the gifts each has been given and encourage each other to use those in our home, in our church, and in our world. Our approach to *who* takes on *what* is based on gifts divinely given to us, not any enslaving ideas the culture or some churches perpetuate about gender. And we honor the fact that the Holy Spirit speaks to both of us about different actions our family should take.

When I first told Rick I felt the Spirit leading us to grow our family through international adoption, He did not question my ability to hear correctly from our Heavenly Father. He quickly responded, "Yes, let's do it!" When Rick felt led to give away more than half of our savings account, I felt a twinge of fear and reluctance, but then submitted those feelings to the Spirit and agreed that we could practice the radical generosity we were being called to. We listen to each other and the Holy Spirit. If we have a differing view, then we wait until the Holy Spirit shines more light on the subject. We seek God until we come to unity in what He is saying to us as a couple. God uses one to confirm and clarify what the other has heard.

Rick and I have cultivated this closeness with trust, particularly trusting what the Holy Spirit speaks to the other. We have made some crazy, Spirit-led decisions in our seven years of marriage, but every time we had confidence in the fact that we heard clearly from Holy Spirit.

Another reason we've been able to enjoy such closeness, and follow these two biblical ideas expressed in Genesis, is that Rick has never allowed outsiders to take away my authority. Husbands are to love their wives as Christ loves the church, and my husband always says, "Christ died to give the church her authority back." It is not uncommon these days for individuals, certain churches, or society to disrespect the leadership potential of women because of some verses taken out of context and without looking at the whole of Scripture. Anytime someone has tried to limit me in using my gifts or has treated me as unequal in function, Rick has been quick to act and speak in a way that restores my God given office as a priest. He fights for me, and I fight for him because we are warriors together.

And this has serious implications for many aspects of our marriage. First, we thoroughly enjoy each other's companionship. We don't have to dutifully choose to love one another because we're having too much fun. We laugh together, we still have tickle fights, and we sit on our porch and talk together about all our thoughts, emotions, fears, and hopes. We also have great sex. I won't elaborate too much, but I will say our love life is both regular and pleasurable. When you are in bed with someone who you know is committed to you, someone who you know would go to great lengths to protect you, someone who trusts you and encourages your passion, well, sex with that person is nothing short of orgasmic.

Again, I want to reiterate that this does not mean we do not have conflict. We communicate openly if we disagree or feel hurt by the other. Relationships with no conflict are not healthy, nor are relationships with constant conflict. Conflict resolution has to actually be about resolution. When we argue, it does not matter what it is about. The goal is to come together—come to agreement. One or both of us might choose to compromise out of love and respect for the other. We do not designate one of us as the tiebreaker because we ask Holy Spirit to take that position.

I find it so profound that immediately before Paul instructs wives to submit to their husbands and for husbands to love their wives like Christ loves the church, to protect her God given humanity, ability, and priestly position, he describes the real necessity for all believers, regardless of sex, social class or age to submit to one another in reverence to Christ (see Ephesians

5:21). Does this show you what Biblical submission is really about? It is not one person dominating another. It is believers preferring one another over themselves and cooperating with each other to remain in unity in order to function together to accomplish God's purposes.

> *Therefore if you have any encouragement from being united with Christ, if any comfort from his love, if any common sharing in the Spirit, if any tenderness and compassion, then make my joy complete by being like-minded, having the same love, being one in spirit and of one mind. Do nothing out of selfish ambition or vain conceit. Rather, in humility value others above yourself not looking to your own interest but each of you to the interests of others.*

> —PHILIPPIANS 2:1–4

We need to be like-minded in unity, because we are all needed for battle, not against man or people who we don't like, but against spiritual darkness. We can't fight the darkness if we are fighting each other.

> *Finally, be strong in the Lord and in his mighty power. Put on the full armor of God, so that you can take your stand against the devil's schemes. For our struggle is not against flesh and blood, but against the rulers, against the authorities, against the powers of this dark world and against the spiritual forces of evil in the heavenly realms. Therefore put on the full armor of God, so that when the day of evil comes, you may be able to stand your ground, and after you have done everything, to stand.*

> —EPHESIANS 6:10–13

Marriage is not just about sex and babies and happiness, although marriage may include those elements. Marriage is about something much greater, much more eternal. When we marry, we choose the man or woman we want to go to war with. When we select a mate, we select a partner to fight the darkness of this world with. Our marriages are just as much about liberating the captives as they are about companionship. Our marriages are a purposeful way to bring love, peace, and hope to our world.

You hear people talk about how selecting a spouse is the most important decision of your life, and I agree with that. I've worked at two Christian Colleges over the past seven years and I've seen people choose mates out of fear that they won't find someone later in life. They think that perhaps if they don't propose or get a proposal by their senior year, they'll be doomed to a life of singleness. If you are single, remember that Paul calls it a gift (see 1 Corinthians 7:7). Find out all the adventure God has for you as a single person! Singles are free to do some things that married people cannot. I have many friends that waited years after graduation before marrying because they did not want to settle for less than God's best, and never have I ever heard them say they wish they had not waited. Getting married right after college is not wrong either. Rick and I married seven days after I graduated from college and have never wished we waited till later. We were ready to start our lives together. The important thing is that you know you're entering a healthy commitment with someone who loves and honors you, and that you're both ready to fight together, side by side to bring light into the darkness. While you are single remember that you have a family in God. Find partnerships with your believing friends to also bring light into the darkness.

I had somewhat of an identity crisis after my freshman year of college, just a few months after Rick and I had been dating. I felt the Holy Spirit leading me in a process of self-discovery and part of that meant giving up some leadership positions I held on campus. I felt like those things defined me, and that without the titles I was not worth much. I told Rick that I needed to talk out some of my feelings, and it was the first time I ever cried in front of him. I remember telling him, "If these responsibilities aren't a part of me anymore than I'm just Maggie." In shock he responded, "Just Maggie? I love just Maggie!"

And ten years later I'm still just Maggie, and he is still just Rick. There's no doubt that even after seeing each other on our absolute worst days, we're even crazier about each other now. I think back to that moment at the concert when Rick chipped his tooth, and consider how we've partnered together since then, and I'm left with this sound conclusion that the journey is both fun and significant. The adventure takes on a new level of purpose, excitement, and impact when you have a likeminded, intimately connected partner who's just as committed to the adventure of bringing light into the darkness.

Reflections

1. What are some ideas you currently have about the marriage relationship that might not be coming from our Heavenly Father?

2. In thinking about companionship and Kingdom building as two very important elements to Christian marriage, what are some things you can do personally to prepare for or improve that relationship?

3. If you are not married yet, do you consider singleness a gift? Why or why not? How can you make the most of your time as a single individual?

Meditation

Consider Ephesians 6:10–13 and ask Holy Spirit for patience to wait for the man or woman who will make a good warrior partner.

NOTES

ADVENTURE AVAILABLE

CHAPTER 8

Enduring for Miles

My freshman year of college I resolved to not gain what some call the "freshman fifteen." I did not think I needed to lose weight but I certainly did not want to pack on any extra pounds. I liked my physical appearance. I did not have any real insecurity in the looks department and I did not want that to change.

I did the only thing I knew to do—I ran. A lot of people hate running, but I never have. When I played basketball in high school I actually liked running sprints. Somehow those short burst of speed assured me I was working hard, getting more competitive, growing in health. When I got cut from the team my Junior year I was so devastated about not being with my teammates anymore I forgot all about my love of the run.

So I started to run/walk on the main road by campus. I would go anywhere from two miles to eventually five miles, three to four times a week. I joined an intramural team and started playing basketball and ultimate Frisbee a few evenings a week. I also took a bet from a friend that I could go without sweets and soda for a few months—a bet I won. I weighed

142 pounds at the beginning of freshman year and by summer break I was down to 122 pounds. Twenty pounds shed all in an attempt to *prevent* average college weight gain! I did not starve myself. I did not get on a scale every day or even every month. I did not count calories or feel bad if I needed to occasionally skip a run to study. I just cut out sugary beverages and snacks and lived actively. For most people this strategy will work to help keep them at a healthy weight and fitness. If, however, this is not working for you, consult a doctor—let them know your struggle and get a complete check-up.

Our Heavenly Father gives us good gifts and we get the honor of caring for those gifts. A steward is someone who cares for another's property. Stewardship means the activity or job of protecting and being responsible for something. We steward our time, our energy, our resources, our money, our possessions, and even our physical bodies. We're only given one body, and if we want to live in adventure with Jesus, we need a body that is up for the tasks ahead. Eating good, nutritious food is choosing to energize with the best fuel. Exercising and staying active is choosing to strengthen the vessel by which we carry the good news. When people dismiss healthy eating and activity as some kind of excuse for vanity, they miss out on the opportunity to prepare our bodies just like we prepare our hearts and mind for adventure and partnership with Jesus.

God loves to give us good gifts—this is such an overwhelming beautiful part of His nature. He also delights in teaching us how to properly care for the gifts He lavishes on us. Our physical bodies are no exception.

Consistently indulging in fat, sugar, gluten, meats pumped with hormones, and alcohol can hurt our bodies in a way that also negatively affects our emotions and dulls our passion. Sadly, being overweight or even obese is too prevalent today. Our choices about what we put in our bodies have a profound impact on our risk for disease, depression, and even death.

College students sometime engage in very risky behaviors that profoundly impact their overall health and well-being. Binge drinking may be one of the most harmful habits. Over half a million college students are injured or die every year from alcohol related incidents. Binge drinking is associated with poor grades, increased chances for being a victim of sexual assault, and poor self-esteem.

I think our Creator made fermented drink for our pleasure. He's a good God and likes for us to have fun. But He wants us to experience the fullness of joy *and* He wants us to stay safe from harm. Scripture tells us many times that drunkenness and gluttony is for fools. This is not because He never wants us to consume alcohol or candy bars. This is because He wants us to have a full, long life with Him. He's not trying to suck the fun out of life. Quite the contrary! He wants us to have a satisfying life, and certain habitual indulgences will really get in the way of that. I'm well aware that some in the Body of Christ adhere to a strict abstinence of alcohol, and I respect that. Others feel the liberty to drink responsively. But we can all agree that binge-drinking, underage drinking, and consistently overindulging in alcohol are both unsafe and unhealthy.

We cannot control all aspects of our health. We all know beautifully healthy people who become ill without any kind of explanation. But that does not change the fact that we can control a great deal of what happens with our health by simply choosing to use wisdom about what we eat and drink and to finding fun ways to stay active and exercise.

My good friends, Shane and Nicole, serve on my church's pastoral leadership team, but they also run a gym out of their garage. Shane is a certified physical trainer and Nicole is a nutritionist. They do not work with professional athletes trying to win the next cross-fit games. They serve the everyday men and women trying to change the pattern of unhealthy choices they've made for years. Their slogan is "My body, His temple" because they feel a real calling to help see people's health, energy and self-worth restored. They want believers to be equipped with a physical body that keeps up with the adventures ahead.

In the Psalms it speaks about our Heavenly Father preparing a banquet table for us. He longs for us to feast and drink of His goodness. He wants us to be in a place to experience deep satisfaction and joy. It says our cups will overflow at His table. Everything He gives is good. He wants us to taste the fruits of the Spirit: love, joy, peace, patience, goodness, kindness, faithfulness, gentleness, and self-control. He wants us to live in a place of rest, not worry. He wants to restore us in every way we need restoring.

King David, the creative psalmist, knew this truth deeply. He had tasted of sumptuous banquets; he had also experienced the extravagant love and grace of his Heavenly Father. His description of the House of the Lord points us to this life of beautiful abundance.

> *The Lord is my shepherd, I lack nothing.*
>   *He makes me lie down in green pastures,*
> *he leads me beside quiet waters,*
>   *he refreshes my soul.*
> *He guides me along the right paths*
>   *for his name's sake.*
> *Even though I walk*
>   *through the darkest valley,*
> *I will fear no evil,*
>   *for you are with me;*
> *your rod and your staff,*
>   *they comfort me.*
> *You prepare a table before me*
>   *in the presence of my enemies.*
> *You anoint my head with oil;*
>   *my cup overflows.*
> *Surely your goodness and love will follow me*
>   *all the days of my life,*
> *and I will dwell in the house of the Lord*
>   *forever.*

—PSALM 23:1–6

Provision. Protection. Rejuvenation. Satisfaction. Comfort even in the toughest of trials. Fearlessness. Fullness. Blessing. Abundance of goodness and love. These are not just the ramblings of a romantic. David describes the reality of life with an extravagantly loving God. Scripture tells us that David was a man after God's own heart; this is clearly why He can so beautifully describe the Father's heart toward His children.

In the book *The Hunger Games: Catching Fire*, Susanne Collins describes the elitist of The Capitol participating in an odd ritual. At a grand party they eat all kinds of delicious foods and then drink a small tonic that makes them sick so their bellies can make room for more food, and they go on eating and puking and eating and puking. It is truly a revolting scene for the protagonists who know people who are actually without enough food, going hungry.

I cannot help but wonder if we sometimes treat our own bodies this haphazardly. Most of us do not throw up to make room for more, but how many of us leave no room for the best? How many of us, like Esau who traded his birthright for a bowl of stew, exchange what is good for a lifetime with what looks appealing right now? This perhaps is why hooking up and sleeping with whoever is willing is becoming so much more common among young adults. What we have to realize is that in the Kingdom if we ever forfeit an indulgence, it is only to create room for something way more fun, satisfying, and purposeful.

Binge drinking, sleeping around, chain smoking, using recreational drugs, overindulging in sugary and fatty foods, and spending all your free time binge watching TV on your couch have some momentary pleasures associated with them. But what are you forfeiting if you choose these things? Not only are they damaging in themselves, but the time wasted in negative behaviors, could have been spent on activities to make your life better—make this world better.

Our Heavenly Father does not want you to suffer the consequences of these behaviors. He does not want you dealing with an unwanted pregnancy, STDs, cirrhosis of the liver, criminal charges, heart problems, obesity, or depression. He wants you to enjoy life to the fullest, because He is head over heels crazy in love with you.

The truth is we can only take in so much, and what we take in serves as the fuel for our lives, for our calling. If we take in primarily what leaves us feeling sluggish and in dire need for nap, we have little room for quality nutrition. If we know our energy, our mood, and our health is impacted by the food and drink we consume, why would we not make the most room for what is good for us? Why would we not steward our bodies just like we steward our time and our finances?

I felt so good after I lost those twenty pounds. I could not really believe I was so satisfied with my prior health habits. For one, I looked very different. I never looked fat before, but I certainly could see the extra, unnecessary fat on my body when I look back at the photos. I had little rolls under my chin when I smiled. My pants were two sizes bigger. But besides liking my new, fitter self, I felt better. I liked that I could go out and run for five miles without taking a walking break. I liked that I was still sprinting in the second half of a Frisbee match. I enjoyed sleeping better and having more energy.

A few years after college graduation, I embarked on a new fitness goal. Rick and I signed up for a half marathon, a 13.1 mile footrace in Atlanta, Georgia. Going from running five miles to thirteen seemed pretty tough, but the challenge also was too intriguing to pass up. I downloaded a beginner plan from the Internet and over the course of about twelve weeks gradually built up my mileage. My good friend, and now favorite running buddy, Becki, trained with me. We made our long runs quality time together, and our friendship grew. We ran the race together, even though she could have run much faster. She liked the teamwork and did not mind going at my slower pace. The cool thing is we still race together. Our first race was in March of 2010 and we went back to Atlanta that next year to improve our time. We did shorter races together too. She helped me with speed and paced me in some ten-kilometer distance events. Five years after our inaugural event we again went back to Atlanta, except this time we ran the full marathon, all 26.2 miles.

The author of Hebrews uses this beautiful illustration of life with Jesus:

> *Therefore, since we are surrounded by such a great cloud of witnesses, let us throw off everything that hinders and the sin that so easily entangles. And let us run with perseverance the race marked out for us, fixing our eyes on Jesus, the pioneer and perfecter of faith. For the joy set before him he endured the cross, scorning its shame, and sat down at the right hand of the throne of God. Consider him who endured such opposition from sinners, so that you will not grow weary and lose heart.*
>
> —HEBREWS 12:1–3

Life, in many ways, is like a race, requiring strength and endurance. Though Jesus is always enough, He created us to run with other witnesses, those who can encourage us, keep us on track, and motivate us not to throw in the towel. In my best races I have run with a pacer, most of the time Rick or Becki. Something about having someone by your side helps you press on, even when you want to stop and take a breather.

You see, we are all participating in an endurance event. The race just serves as a metaphor for this journey we are on with Jesus. He is by our side, pacing us because He really knows what endurance means. He took on the ultimate perseverance challenge and thus knows exactly how to encourage us, motivate us, sustain us, and empower us. Caring for our physical bodies is choosing to do our best for an endurance event. Otherwise we might find ourselves ready to quit after the first leg of the race. If we want to have adventures for longer than a day, we need to think ahead and train to endure for miles.

Taking care of our physical bodies is about much more than longevity and happiness. It's about how we bring holiness here on earth just as it is in heaven. In this partnership with Jesus we want to finish the race. When you prepare for a footrace you prepare your body for the event. When you partner with Christ, you align your heart, mind, body, and soul with His will. When you partner with Christ you care for your body, just like you do your heart, mind, and soul because you recognize that it too is a gift to enjoy and steward. You cannot say that any part of you is not valuable, because all of you is needed to join with Christ in all the adventures that lie ahead.

Reflection

1. Are you stewarding your physical health well? If not, what are some unhealthy habits you would like to eliminate from your life? What are some healthy habits you would like to take on?

2. What barriers might you face in this process of healthy living? How can you overcome these challenges?

3. Are there friends around you that might want to help you in your journey to caring for your physical health? Who might be able to run this race with you?

Meditation

Consider again the passage in Hebrews 12 and think about some of the long-term goals you have for yourself. Ask the Holy Spirit to show you how stewarding your health will help give you strength and endurance for those life aspirations.

NOTES

CHAPTER 9

Generous on Every Occasion

ick and I were both working at our alma mater when
Rick began to feel more and more that we were being called to be more involved with ministry at United
Assembly, our church in Seneca, South Carolina (see: http://
unitedassembly.com/). It was about thirty-five miles from our
on-campus apartment. He had planned to interview for the position of the associate pastor, but we decided on something
that seemed pretty crazy at the time. We were going to move to
Seneca regardless of the interview outcome. We just knew the
Holy Spirit was calling us to make our home there.

So I did what came naturally—I started watching HGTV
every spare moment of my life. I watched shows about buying
a home, shows about remodeling homes, shows about how to
make your house look like the photos in magazines instead of
a dwelling that is actually lived in—if it revolved around home-
ownership, I devoured it. It was kind of an obsessive hobby.
But I was just really excited about our first home. We'd lived
in an apartment in Seneca our first month married. We left for
an apartment attached to a residence hall that housed 101 male

underclassmen when Rick was hired as the Resident Area Director at our alma mater, Emmanuel College. Needless to say, the thought of our own private space was very exciting!

When it came time to get pre-qualified for a home loan, I was quite perplexed at what we were told we could spend. We both worked for the college, earning very modest salaries. I think the mortgage which the bank pre-qualified us for would have been just a little over fifty percent of what we made each month, which I thought was ridiculous. Even though I had been quite enthralled by all the TV shows about buying the perfect home, I could not help but think this kind of purchase could suck all the fun out of life. No more eating out or treating friends to lunch when convenient. No more one night get-a-ways. No more flexibility for random gift giving. No more room to save twenty percent of our income like we had been. Buying a house for the amount the bank allowed might have meant a really fine house, but it also would have meant a really restricted life.

When we met with our realtor we told her we were only willing to buy a home with a mortgage that was about half of what the bank approved us for. We found a beautiful home in the historic district that had recently been remodeled, so it was not a money pit. It was also right in the heart of downtown, really close to the railroad tracks (which did not scare us because we are both very heavy sleepers). It certainly had its quirks and imperfections: blue carpet on just the stairs cases, no garage, and a pretty small yard that could not seem to grow grass because of all the shade from the pecan trees. But it had tons of space, needed no major repairs, a balcony off the upstairs master bedroom, and best of all our monthly mortgage was reasonable. This is where we chose to start our new season of ministry. And not once have we regretted opting to spend less than the bank told us we could!

A few years down the road when we were about to become parents, we knew we needed a car that was a bit more conducive to fitting in a car seat or two. I, of course, began looking at nearby dealers and Autotrader and suddenly become quite enthralled with the Hyundai Santa Fe. It was sporty and fun—the perfect vehicle. My mind was made up that we should buy this make and model.

But Rick's grandfather had several cars he did not use often, and when he found out we were in the market, he offered to sell us his 2004 Toyota Camry that was in mint condition with only 60,000 miles. He even said we could make interest free payment on it since he knew we had spent the majority of our savings on the down payment of our house. Not only that, but his sale price was about two-thirds the value of the car. For me there was just one problem. The car was gold.

I know that may sound silly to some, but I really wanted a car that fit my personality. I also wanted dual air control. If I was going to be toting around kids, I wanted to do it in style. This deal did not seem sweet. I wanted to decline the offer and buy the more expensive, more fancy Hyundai with loads of interest and a much higher price tag, until I started thinking about the month-to-month impact. Again, looking at what might have to go if we bought the more expensive car, I had a change of heart. The expensive car might have been more stylish, but it would also suck more freedom out of life. We bought the gold Camry from Rick's grandpa and again, never regretted that decision once.

Everybody has to make these kinds of decisions about major purchases and what will be allowed in their monthly expenses. These choices have very real, natural consequences, but I think sometimes we fail to see the Kingdom opportunities that lie with the way we treat our finances. The Bible talks a lot about money, and the closer Rick and I have followed Christ, the more importance we give to freedom to be generous with others, simplicity, and stewardship.

One thing we've found very helpful in managing our money in a way that reflects the love of the Father is to be guided by principles rather than very strict rules. A lot of people live by extremes when it comes to the stewardship of their finances. Some live by very strict rules and formulas that hinder their ability to make radical generosity possible on a regular basis. Others live without guidelines and just let their money control them instead of the other way around. Neither of these approaches leaves room for Spirit-led management of the resources given to us by our generous Heavenly Father.

I read a finance book recently that I really liked. It stressed the value of becoming debt free, even free from a mortgage, and saving for retirement and children's college expenses. It had a lot of good points that appealed to me, one being the freedom to choose a career regardless of the salary because of the absence of debt. It had a lot of ideas that I would consider Kingdom focused. There was only one problem, this guide to financial freedom talked very little of generosity to those outside your own family. In fact, it did not even recommend being generous with others until one had eliminated all debt. This book was full of wisdom, but it lacked the freedom to make radical choices to show love and generosity to others.

In my work with college students and young adults, I very often observe the opposite. I see individuals racking up debt, not planning at all how to manage their monthly income, and this leads to the same problem: an inability to be generous and a general lack of financial freedom. In my observations, I see two major themes contributing to this careless use of money- insecurity and impatience. Making a purchase should not be about status or a desire for others to see you as important. Having to have a three-hundred-dollar purse or a thirty thousand dollar sports car to dazzle and impress others is wasteful vanity. Making purchases you cannot actually afford, rather than taking the time to save up for things you want, demonstrates a lack of discipline. Choices made out of insecurity or impatience do not typically lead to radical generosity.

There must be a balance between the strict rules and the careless choices about money. Rick and I have had to work together to find the right balance for our family, but we go often to this verse:

Remember this: Whoever sows sparingly will also reap sparingly, and whoever sows generously will also reap generously. Each of you should give what you have decided in your heart to give, not reluctantly or under compulsion, for God loves a cheerful giver. And God is able to bless you abundantly, so that in all things at all times, having all that you need, you will abound in every good work. As it is written:

"They have freely scattered their gifts to the poor; their righteousness endures forever."

Now he who supplies seed to the sower and bread for food will also supply and increase your store of seed and will enlarge the harvest of your righteousness. You will be enriched in every way so that you can be generous on every occasion, and through us your generosity will result in thanksgiving to God.

This service that you perform is not only supplying the needs of the Lord's people but is also overflowing in many expressions of thanks to God. Because of the service by which you have proved yourselves, others will praise God for the obedience that accompanies your confession of the gospel of Christ, and for your generosity in sharing with them and with everyone else. And in their prayers for you their hearts will go out to you, because of the surpassing grace God has given you. Thanks be to God for his indescribable gift!

—2 CORINTHIANS 9:6–15

The way we use our money should be a reflection of our Heavenly Father's love, which draw others into this love. This love is not exclusively for our immediate family members, nor should it exclude them. Using our money to show love to our kids certainly includes giving them good gifts, saving for their futures, and desiring to leave them a generous inheritance. But loving our kids also means teaching them the importance of radical generosity and making sacrifices, sacrifices they feel, so others can be blessed.

I felt led at one point to give away the car I had driven in college. We knew a young lady from church who was in her last year of college, and she was borrowing vehicles from friends just to get to class. It was stressful for her, and I very strongly felt that God wanted us to give her our car. We were in the process of shopping for another family vehicle because a drunk driver smashed our gold Camry. We knew it made more sense to trade in the old car, but we allowed Holy Spirit's prompting to guide us in giving it away.

We have a really good friend whose vehicle needed some serious repairs, and Rick really wanted to help with the expenses. But we were in the process of saving for my maternity leave at the time and knew we really could not spare any from our savings account. We brainstormed and decided to sell some of our guest bedroom furniture on Craigslist. We gave our friend that money to help with the cost of the repairs. That is what the early church did. When someone had a need, they sold things they did not really need to help provide for their loved ones, their beloved community.

Do not think for a second that Rick and I don't spend money on us. We feel the freedom to treat ourselves. Life in the

Kingdom is about freedom, not restriction. A few years back Rick told me he wanted to start saving up to buy a house on Lake Keowee. I thought this was frivolous at first. But Rick was not after status or prestige. He wanted fun and enjoyment, for us as a couple, for our kids, and for our friends. After thinking about it for about a year, we did develop a long-term plan to save up for a down payment on what we think will be a foreclosure on the lake. We're not opposed to enjoying this life because we know God gives us gifts so we can enjoy them!

Rick and I are generous and feel free to have fun because we have experienced how generous our Heavenly Father is toward us. Time and time again we have received such beautiful gifts from Him. When we consider everything good in our lives and recognize that it all comes from God, that transformational love propels us to be generous too. We are motivated to give generously and we are motivated to enjoy this life with those we love. In this adventure we have choices to make with our money that will draw others closer to the Father's love and make this life more fun and fulfilling. If God is the giver of good gifts, we steward those gifts by both enjoying them and by imitating His generosity, so that others may also enjoy the loving provision and generosity of our good and extravagantly loving Heavenly Father.

> *Every good and perfect gift is from above, coming down from the Father of the heavenly lights, who does not change like shifting shadows.*
>
> —JAMES 1:17

Refection

1. Do you tend to hoard your treasures or spend impulsively? What changes can you make about your spending habits that might help you give more generously?

2. Do you currently budget your money? If not, consider asking someone to help you with monthly budget and long-term saving.

Meditation

Read and re-read James 1. Ask the Holy Spirit to show you all the good gifts you've been given. Thank God for all those blessings. Then ask to be empowered to bless others. Pray and seek direction about a specific person or cause to impact in the immediate future.

NOTES

ADVENTURE AVAILABLE

CHAPTER 10

From A Long Way Off

Before Rick and I even got engaged, we confided in one another that we had a desire to adopt children as well as grow our family biologically. We thought it was a cool thing that we both had such a desire, but later discussed what we considered a practical plan of having bio-babies first (or home-conceived babies as I like to refer to them). My logic was pretty superficial. I wanted to get pregnancy out of the way while I was young enough to recover well from the physical changes that can happen, and then adopt children later in our marriage.

Then some years after getting married, I attended the Catalyst Conference in Atlanta where I got to hear Francis Chan speak. His message was powerful. Essentially he said making disciples is a process of imitating Christ and then leading others to do the same. But in a culture dominated with selfishness, we had an epidemic of people shaping others to be just like them—selfish. Then he got to the main thrust—the mark of a disciple is one who is willing to make Spirit-led decisions, even when they cost us, even when no one else will understand, and even when those decisions go against cultural norms.

As Francis Chan was speaking these words, the Holy Spirit immediately spoke to my heart and confirmed that Rick and I were to adopt, but that we were to start now—earlier than we had planned. Suddenly my heart was filled with love for my first child, a child I did not yet know by name or face. I just knew the Lord was doing something new in my heart, and that He was also doing something beautiful in our family. He was calling us to something untraditional, not completely understood by others, and to a journey not without pain and risk. But I knew it was a Spirit-led move, part of our adventure with our Savior. Even knowing the challenges, how could Rick and I choose normal over this divinely blessed course?

I believe most people have inclinations to live with either safety or stupidity, and neither is healthy. We want to let either logic or thrill direct each step, letting our own thoughts or emotions take the position of God in our lives. But Jesus was not safe or stupid. He took risks all the time. He put Himself in dangerous situations. He chose with great intention His words and actions in every given moment. He was not selfish. He loved to please His Heavenly Father. He did not let fear subdue Him into a safe life, nor did he let carelessness cage him into a reckless life. Jesus lived a brave life, and He calls us to do the same.

Every single person out there has moments of opportunity for bravery, to live the life in communion with God. The safe life and the stupid life are both a result of selfishness. The brave life is one where the love of the Father, the love of fellow brothers and sisters in the faith, and love of the nonbelievers trumps any impulse to be scared or indifferent. Regret accompanies the choices made out of fear and foolishness. Fulfillment accompanies the choices made out of brave partnership with Christ.

When I came home from the conference, I was in tears. I had been listening to Michael Gungor's *Beautiful Things* the entire car ride home from Atlanta, just soaking in God's love for my future child. I immediately told Rick about what Holy Spirit had spoken to me and his response reminded me again of the beautiful gift it is to be partnered with a bold believer. "Let's do it!" He said readily. "I've never wanted a boring family. I want our family to look like the Kingdom of God."

We chose to adopt our first child from Ethiopia. We had done short-term mission work there and loved so many things about the beautiful country, from the strong coffee shared in ceremony with new friends, to the cool, breezy weather. Did some think it very odd for a young, fertile couple to choose adoption? Sure. Did some think it inappropriate to choose to create a multiethnic family? Yep, again. But we did not let that faze or deter us. We were okay with being perceived as weird by some.

In the years leading up to us meeting our son Grady, I faced some painfully tough moments. There was the long wait for a referral. Our court date when we would actually get to meet him face to face was postponed time and time again stretching my ability to endure. My heart ached for the child I knew existed outside of my love and protection. I wanted him near. I longed for him to be home.

I'll never forget meeting Grady for the first time. He cried at the sight of me, reaching back for his affectionate nannies that staffed the orphanage where he spent most of the first year of his life. But I soothed him rather quickly. Maybe he just liked the way I smelled or the playful way I spoke to him. He certainly could not know then how much I loved him, how much I cried for him, how deeply I longed for him to be home in the months, even years before our union. He was finally ours, orphaned no longer.

And in the next few years of my life, Father revealed Himself to me in a greater way as the caring, nurturing, relentless pursuer of His children. It was not until we adopted Grady that I began to get an idea of the depths of the tenacity, the endurance, or the undeniable affection God has toward his children, lost and found. Prior to adopting, when I read the parables about that woman looking for her coin and that shepherd leaving the ninety-nine other sheep to look for the lost one, I did not feel the longing of our Heavenly Father. But after experiencing the urgency, the pain, and the longing to be united with my son, suddenly I felt in tune with Father's heart.

And I've never read the story of the Prodigal Son quite the same way.

> *Jesus continued: "There was a man who had two sons. The younger one said to his father, 'Father, give me my share of the estate.' So he divided his property between them.*

"Not long after that, the younger son got together all he had, set off for a distant country and there squandered his wealth in wild living. After he had spent everything, there was a severe famine in that whole country, and he began to be in need. So he went and hired himself out to a citizen of that country, who sent him to his fields to feed pigs. He longed to fill his stomach with the pods that the pigs were eating, but no one gave him anything.

"When he came to his senses, he said, 'How many of my father's hired servants have food to spare, and here I am starving to death! I will set out and go back to my father and say to him: Father, I have sinned against heaven and against you. I am no longer worthy to be called your son; make me like one of your hired servants.' So he got up and went to his father.

"But while he was still a long way off, his father saw him and was filled with compassion for him; he ran to his son, threw his arms around him and kissed him.

"The son said to him, 'Father, I have sinned against heaven and against you. I am no longer worthy to be called your son.'

"But the father said to his servants, 'Quick! Bring the best robe and put it on him. Put a ring on his finger and sandals on his feet. Bring the fattened calf and kill it. Let's have a feast and celebrate. For this son of mine was dead and is alive again; he was lost and is found.' So they began to celebrate.

—LUKE 15:11–24

The Father, seeing his son from a long way off, runs to embrace his son. I can't hold back the tears when I read that story because I know how that father felt, rejoicing at their much longed for union. Because I had to pray my son home, because I had to prayerfully contend for him, I've experienced just a glimpse of the love our heavenly Father has for His sons and daughters. I know my heavenly Father loves me and pursues me. After all, at one time I was lost. But He chased me, Maggie, His little girl, just like Rick and I chased after Grady, our little boy.

The adventure we embark on with Christ is not dissimilar. We are looking for our lost brothers and sisters. Christ invites us to join with Him in the pursuit. We look for those with no home and with no hope. We look for those filled with despair, overwhelmed with pain. We chase those that run because God knows they belong with Him. They are sons, they are daughters, and the ministry of reconciliation is about bringing them home to a loving Father that refuses to let go of the children He loves so dearly. It does not matter how far away they are. From a long way off, He sees them. And my prayer is that we have eyes to see them too.

Remember again Paul's description of the ministry of reconciliation:

> *God was reconciling the world to himself in Christ, not counting people's sin against them. And he has committed to us the message of reconciliation. We are therefore Christ's ambassadors, as though God were making is appeal through us. We implore you on Christ's behalf: Be reconciled to God.*

—2 CORINTHIANS 5: 19–20

Each of us has a different part to play in the ministry of reconciliation. Some are called to adopt orphaned children. Others are called to love and care for those suffering from disease. Some are called to rescue victims of human trafficking. Others are called to create art that touches the hearts of cultural elites. We are all unique, so we all have a beautifully important role to play, but our purpose is the same. We are on this adventure with Christ to welcome all into the family of God, and to help others experience the good news. There is great sacrifice involved, but there is even more joy.

Grady has been an incredible source of joy in my life. He is absolutely precious to me, Rick, his younger brother Hananiah, and his younger sister Judah. Rick and I do not look back at how much emotional turbulence we went through or how much money we had to raise and think we would have been better off following an easier route. On the contrary—I cannot imagine our family without our eldest child—Grady is our delight! He is special to us and He is special to the Kingdom of God.

Just like Grady has brought so much joy to our lives, the rewards of being believers committed to the ministry of reconciliation are great. Joy is an ever-present reality in the Kingdom of God. Welcoming home our lost brothers and sisters, restoring hope to the brokenhearted, and seeing the sick made well is not without an abundance of joy and celebration. This adventure is not just a risky one—it is a blessed, fun life.

Growing up, my pastor's son A.J. Buffington modeled for me what it meant to live the brave life. And he certainly made it look fun! He was an energetic young man, full of love for His Savior and love for those in need of His Savior's love. Not too long after graduating from college, he went to work for the International Justice Mission, (https://www.ijm.org/) a non-profit organization that pursues justice for victims of human trafficking. A.J. was a smart, charismatic guy with a great sense of humor. He was always saying witty things and making others laugh. He could have chosen a safer path, a job with a higher pay and better benefits. He could have chosen a reckless path and buried his talents away in order to have more time for playing video games and binge drinking. But he partnered with Jesus. He did not want the selfish life. He wanted the adventurous life.

I'll never forget the day my dad called me and told me A.J. had been in a terrible car accident and lost his life. I came home for his funeral, and the church was absolutely packed. Everyone who knew A.J. knew he was an adventurer. No one left that service thinking they wanted to live a safer life or more self-indulgent life. We all walked away hoping we could make a difference in the Kingdom the way A.J. had. I walked away hoping to make every moment in my life count.

Life with Christ is an extraordinary adventure. The ministry of reconciliation is what He calls us to. Though it is not free from pain, suffering, or sacrifice, it is free of regret and full of joy. You never regret bravery, just like you never want less joy. So let us be a generation of believers who refuse to pray insignificant prayers like "Lord keep me safe." Instead let us be a generation praying something much wiser, much more impactful. Every day let our prayer be "Lord, every day I am blessed with breath, give me eyes to see the lost and brokenhearted from a long way off, and help me be brave in the rescue."

Reflection

1. Do you feel prompted by the Holy Spirit to make any adventurous decisions that might not make sense to your friends and family? Describe how you process and practice obedience with these divine leadings?

2. Who are you currently contending for? Do you have brothers and sisters you are actively inviting into the family of God?

Meditation

Re-read the story of the prodigal son. Ask our Heavenly Father to love you and let you see yourself as the one returning. Allow yourself to experience His joy with your return to the family of God.

NOTES

CHAPTER 11

Every Tribe

When I was just a young girl, before even hitting puberty, my dad sat me down for a very important talk. He said one day I was going to want to get married, and he wanted to spell out his criteria for this man I would marry. He told me I had the freedom to marry a man of any color, as long as his heart belonged to Jesus. I did not realize exactly what prompted this speech. I had not really ever thought about what my future husband might look like, or that skin color or nationality was even an issue. This conversation took place when I was around nine years old! And I think at that time I already knew I wanted to marry a man who loved Jesus. But for whatever reason, I always remembered that moment with my father.

It was not too long after that conversation that I was sat down for talk with another relative. This person who loves me a great deal started off in the same way, informing me that one day I would want to get married. Only this time I was cautioned with only one guideline for selecting my lifetime partner. This person wanted me to know that when I chose a mate, I needed to choose someone from "my own kind." Whether or not the guy's heart belonged to Jesus was never mentioned. He just needed to be a white guy. And I too will also always remember that conversation, and the uncomfortable way it made me feel, and that it contradicted what my parents had said.

At age nine, I really didn't know what racism was yet. But my parents knew that racism robs people of their God given dignity and humanity and they tried to set a better example for us by intentionally living and speaking in a way that brings unity rather than division. My dad has relationships with black and Hispanic pastors in our city as well those he meets as he travels to Africa, South America and Asia. He took me to black gospel choir concerts at churches his coworkers attended. My mom was supportive when I joined the black gospel choir at school. They were not going to let any of their children get swept up in the lies that people of different color or culture were inferior. My sisters and I made observations about people who looked differently, spoke differently, people with cultural differences by being around them in real relationships, not by making assumptions after exposure to the media or comments made from those inside our own ethnic group.

In college I learned that many parents did not raise their children like this. This, of course, troubled me. But it was not until Rick and I welcomed Grady into our family that the issue of prejudice and ethnocentrism really began to weigh heavy on my heart. I began to see the desperate need for true adventurers with Christ to take up the work of racial reconciliation in our country.

Adventure with Christ is not just fun, thrill seeking exploits. Life with Christ can at times be dangerously outside our comfort zone. When we say yes to this adventure, it includes defending the defenseless, and much of this task may be uncomfortable, unpopular, and even unsafe. It requires deep, reflective self-examination with Heavenly Father. This examination is not condemning, but it is necessary. We open ourselves up to a Heavenly Father who loves us and allow Him to gently purge us of all thoughts and patterns of thinking that do not come from Him. If we want to follow Him on this journey, we cannot afford to think in ways He does not think. We cannot mistreat people that God created and that Jesus died for, nor can we stand by while others mistreat them. Negative thoughts lead to sinful actions in opposition to God's will, which cripple our efforts to bring light and life to the families, churches, and communities around us.

This self-examination process can be painful. Not only do we have to repent of hurtful thoughts and deeds, we also have to come to terms with the fact that someone we love taught us those things. God does not teach us that certain people are better than others—people do. But not just any people—often times we find the origin of some of our most damaging assumptions to be mothers, fathers, teachers, pastors, mentors—people we love and respect.

The beautiful thing about life in the Kingdom is that we don't stop loving the perpetuators of hate or prejudice. Instead we see God's love for them and see the work to gently pull them closer to the truth. We do not condemn; we usher others into liberating truth.

Not too long after the death of unarmed Eric Garner, I was driving to work and I started thinking about a time when I was seventeen years old. I got pulled over for doing 55 mph in a 35 mph zone. I could have been hauled off to jail. I could have been fined a hefty sum. But I cried and told the officer how sorry I was, and he let me go with a warning. That story kept running through my mind as I considered what might happen to Grady in the same situation. My sweet, kind boy might be presumed dangerous. And when I pulled into my parking space at work I started bawling.

I cried because I was scared. Prior to adopting Grady racist ideas held by the whites I deemed ignorant in my community were just sad, because those people were stuck in their unenlightened ways of thinking, missing out on the potential for beautiful relationships. Now racism was a threat to my children's health and safety, not just their ability to succeed. But I felt the Holy Spirit gently convict me, speaking to my spirit, "You are not called to live a life of fear. You are called to be an agent of hope."

One of my good friends from high school called me not too recently to complain to me about how racist her mom had acted towards her brother's new finance. Her brother got engaged to a black woman, and her mom was not approving at all, making family get-togethers uncomfortable. After my friend described the frustrations with her mom's line of thinking she made a comment that took me by surprise. She said, "I do not understand how my mom can dislike this girl so much. She is so sweet and kind. She's really white."

My friend, a woman who loved the Lord and knew prejudice was wrong, still saw this situation through a very distorted lens. She thought this black woman was really "white" because she is likable and relatable and kind. What she meant was that she wasn't culturally different—she was just like my friend and her people. And this is why we have such difficulty today with real reconciliation. My generation knows racism is wrong, but we have not let go of the baggage from the years of being taught that my group (people who look like me, talk like me, and value what I value) is the only group that is worthy of respect and inclusion.

When you learn something so wrong for so long, it is a desperately difficult task to unlearn these ideas. In fact, I'm very convinced that the only way to cleanse our hearts and minds of prejudice is to allow the transforming power of the Holy Spirit to heal our thought patterns and heart's desires.

It is hard for me to write about this topic, partially because I still have some baggage, some fears of my own. But it is also hard because I want solutions now, solutions I don't yet have. I want a practical, step by step plan to see a world where both of my sons are treasured, or at least respected, *or at the very least safe*. But after spending time in prayer, asking God for his thoughts, He flooded my heart and mind with a prophetic declaration, a real hope for the future, and guide for the present. This is what God spoke to my heart to share:

Our powerful, almighty God is ushering the Body of Christ into a new season characterized by love, honor, gentleness, and power. He is transforming His people into beautiful leaders who observe carefully, speak wisely, and act bravely in defense of the defenseless. The young will long for freedom for those in physical captivity, spiritual bondage, and under societal persecution. The old will see the dreams of their youth resurrected, their hearts broken for the suffering, and their courage increased tenfold.

Those who love the Heavenly Father, follow after Jesus, and continually invite the empowering of the Holy Spirit into their lives will be a part of a great banquet feast. And as we feast on the goodness of God we will usher others to the banqueting table. Those who had been excluded because of class or color or culture will be embraced with open arms and given seats of honor and abounding love.

Those who have enslaving ideas, thinking about others in ways God never would, their minds will be renewed. Their hearts will be restored. Their spirit will be transformed by life-giving truth. That divine truth will literally set free those who have been slaves for centuries. They shall know the freedom of the Father and shower others with such freedom.

We will have eyes to see injustice. No longer will anyone yoked with Christ be able to turn a blind eye to the suffering of our spiritual brothers and sisters. Not only will we see with open eyes, but also our words, full of grace, will lead others out of their spiritual blindness. We will carry the power to transform the oppressors into liberators. Even the hardest of hearts will be softened. Even those bound up in religion and pride will be set free and propelled into a life of love and humility. Our actions, full of courage, will protect the oppressed. We will co-labor with Christ in a movement to defend the defenseless.

This will also be a season of beautiful reconciliation. Those who have carried hurts for years and years will trade their mourning for joy, their pain for healing, and their anger for a righteous thirst for justice and compassion. The powers of hell and darkness will tremble when we seek to forgive those who have done great injustices against us. God is releasing in us the power to forgive those who have caused the most terrible of hurts, and we will then lead a movement that will break the chains of unforgiveness in our generation. By radically loving those who persecute us, we will bring a Kingdom revival and culture of peace and honor to our children and our children's children.

We will be a people who worship the Lord in unity. As one body, every tribe and every tongue, every clan and every culture shall love and honor one another. We will respect our differences, love our uniqueness, and treasure the power of collaborating together to bring others into the light, the truth of the Gospel. We will be a loving family. We will be a mighty army. This calling will not be fulfilled by the indifferent or the lazy or the weak. This is the path for the passionate disciple, the courageous warrior, and the surrendered servant. Only the transformational work of Holy Spirit can ready us. And we cannot be prepared without giving up our emotional baggage, our past hurts, the lessons not learned from Christ; all these things must be laid down. And He who is faithful and powerful and loving will take this baggage and replace it with riches and gifts. Instead of insecurity we will know perfect love. Instead of pride and religion we will possess a gentle humility and total freedom. Instead of hate we will carry compassion. When we surrender to the will of God, we will be changed, and our families, our churches, our communities, even our world will experience beloved unity.

May we all surrender to the transformational power of our living God, creator of all mankind. May we invite Him every day to cleanse the thoughts of our hearts by the inspiration of the Holy Spirit, so we might perfectly love Him and worship Him by loving all His beautiful children.

Reflection

1. Do you have thoughts about people of different ethnicities or cultures that are not from Heavenly Father. What are they?

2. How can you begin replacing any prejudice thoughts with heavenly thoughts?

3. Do you need to forgive those who have treated you or your loved one's unjustly? Are you ready to ask Jesus to help you release your hurts and sorrows?

Meditation

Ask the Holy Spirit to fill your heart with a desire for love, peace, and justice. Ask for supernatural power to renew your mind and for your heart to be filled with feelings of compassion.

NOTES

ADVENTURE AVAILABLE

CHAPTER 12

How to Build a Fire

I have known from a very young age the merciful and loving nature of my Heavenly Father, with one slight but ever so significant exception. I believed He loved the lost. I believed His heart was full of compassion toward the sick and the broken-hearted. I believed He treasured all his children expect one—me. Without really recognizing this flaw in my theology, somehow I had internalized this misconception that God had a mean streak, an untrustworthy withholding attitude toward me. But because He loved me beyond measure, He refused to let me sit in this place of distorted perception.

Growing up and even in college, I loved corporate worship. But when Rick and I started going to United I did not feel the freedom to connect with my Heavenly Father the way I used to. I honestly had a bad attitude about the format and the freedom. First of all, worship typically lasted over an hour. How could I engage for that amount of time? Secondly, sometimes during worship people would operate in supernatural gifts like prophesy and speaking or singing in a heavenly language and interpretation of that word or song. Honestly, I thought that was a bit awkward. I did not doubt the validity of the gifts. I just wanted to be comfortable.

One month after we brought Grady home from Ethiopia, we found out we were pregnant. God told me that this child was going to be a worshiper, and suddenly my heart began to change. I actually liked that we did not cut off worship after thirty minutes. I wanted to sing and lavish love on my Heavenly Father. I wanted to profess my love and adoration to Him. And I wanted to do it for an hour during Sunday morning service and at home in our "upper room." I found once again this beautiful connecting point with my Heavenly Father. I loved corporate worship again.

On January 21, after thirty-seven hours of labor, we welcomed our second son, Hananiah Redding Turner, into our family. When he was born, and in the months afterwards, I experienced some crazy emotions. I could have explained them away by saying it was just my hormones changing, but I knew my heart was really just crying out for intimacy with God, and I clearly sensed Him drawing me closer. It was time to deal with these false ideas about how He felt towards me. I now had two sons, and still felt I had no clue how to be a mom. I was mourning the freedom Rick and I had previously, when it was just the two of us, and feeling immensely guilty about the fact that I was regularly wondering if becoming parents was a mistake. I was hurting. I was utterly vulnerable. And that is actually a great time to let God do healing work in your life.

One week after Han was born, Rick gave me a book to read

by Graham Cooke that posed a very beautiful question. Cooke wrote that so often times in trials and challenges we want to ask God "Why is this happening to me?" but really we should be asking, "Who do you want to be for me right now?" And that is what I did. I asked Holy Spirit to speak clearly to my heart and answer my question, "Who do you want to be for me right now?"

He immediately spoke to my spirit and said, "I want to be your Mother." I immediately thought that was a strange response, but He began to make it more clear to my spirit. He saw my present need for comfort and nurture. As I had just begun this hugely important role of caring for my sweet sons, He wanted to care for me. He eased my guilt. He filled me with hope. He gave me rest. He showed me I had everything I needed to raise my children because I was made in His image, and he was big enough to be both Mother and Father to me. He invented the concept of motherhood, and everything in my nature that would make me a good mom came from my Creator.

My heart was restored to a place where I loved to worship, and my spirit was receiving the care that drew me back to a place of intimacy. For the first time in my life I did not doubt God's goodness. I always thought God just did good things. I discovered He does not just randomly commit acts of kindness, but that everything about Him is good in every moment. Holy Spirit was building a fire in my heart, a longing for closeness with Him, and an equally deep desire to help others understand His goodness and powerful love.

Worship often ignites the fire in our hearts. When you do not feel close to God—start worshiping Him! Tell Him why you love Him. Sing new songs to Him. Write letters and poetry to Him. Dance or paint for Him. Find ways to praise Him with your mind and heart and see the sparks fly! My husband has preached many times that worship leads to intimacy, intimacy leads to revelation, and revelation encourages deeper worship. I've seen this in my own life. It is a beautiful cycle. If you want to burn with passion for your Savior, worship will cultivate deep intimacy.

Satan does not like for us to worship or experience intimacy with our Heavenly Father. So don't be surprised when you are attacked with his lies that cause feelings of resistance to worship. Whatever plans the enemy has to thwart our closeness with God—God always uses them to draw us even closer, after dispelling the lies and giving us even deeper revelation about His love and power.

When Han was just eight months old, our church had its annual deacon and elder retreat. One of our elders prayed for me and prophesied that I would give birth to another child. Included in the prophecy from God was a word that I might get some bad news from a doctor in the near future, but that I should not worry. What this elder did not know is that I was experiencing some abnormal bleeding and pain pretty regularly. My aliments were not typical postpartum issues. I thought *maybe I do need to go to the doctor!*

My doctor scheduled an ultrasound and discovered a very

large mass on my right ovary. Because it was not there when Han was born and because of the symptoms I was having, my doctor recommended surgery right away. She told me because of the size of the mass there was a very slim chance I would be able to keep the ovary, and she told me they would do a biopsy to find out if it was cancerous. My surgery was scheduled for December 5, 2014.

Right there in my doctor's office I started crying. Just weeks before I had run my first sub-2 hour half marathon. I was in perfect health. I was stronger than I had ever been, not just physically but spiritually too. How could it be possible that I could have cancer at twenty-nine? I only had two questions for her: "Will there be a good chance for future pregnancies?" And, "If everything is okay can I still train for a full marathon in March?" She surprised me with answering yes to both, so I felt a bit more reassured.

In the days leading up to surgery, I had myself convinced that I did have cancer. I thought perhaps because I had never gone through anything extremely traumatic or challenging that this was my time to learn to suffer for the Gospel. I was truly scared. I expected the worst.

A couple weeks before the surgery, the same elder prayed over me for complete healing. And she told me after she prayed that Holy Spirit impressed upon her heart that I was already healed, and the sizable mass was no longer there.

I absolutely did not believe her.

I had been bracing myself for the worst, and I was not about to let my guard down. I did not even write about her prayer in my prophetic journal. I could not accept this word over my life. I knew something was wrong. I knew I was going to suffer like I had never suffered before.

I cried before surgery. I had never been put under before, and it was a little unnerving. My doctor told me if surgery took a long time that it would be a good thing because it would likely mean they were able to save the ovary. But if the surgery was quick it meant they realized as soon as they opened me it up it was a lost cause. I woke up less than thirty minutes later.

As soon as I saw the large hospital clock I knew I was down an ovary. But something was wrong. I had a small incision on left side and one in my belly button, but nothing on my right side. For a second I thought maybe they took the wrong ovary!

Rick quickly filled me in. There was nothing there. No mass. No cancer. Whatever was on my ovary before was there no longer. I was totally and completely healed.

In a year's time I grew to love spending hours worshiping and praying in the spirit. I connected with the Father closer than I ever had before. And then I received the most awesome gift, a revelation of His love for me—and also a revelation of His power to change any situation. Suddenly, the only thing worth being overwhelmed by was His love, joy, peace, and hope. I began meditating on this Scripture passage:

When God made his promise to Abraham, since there was no one greater for him to swear by, he swore by himself, saying, "I will surely bless you and give you many descendants." And so after waiting patiently, Abraham received what was promised.

People swear by someone greater than themselves, and the oath confirms what is said and puts an end to all argument. Because God wanted to make the unchanging nature of his purpose very clear to the heirs of what was promised, he confirmed it with an oath. God did this so that, by two unchangeable things in which it is impossible for God to lie, we who have fled to take hold of the hope set before us may be greatly encouraged. We have this hope as an anchor for the soul, firm and secure. It enters the inner sanctuary behind the curtain, where our forerunner, Jesus, has entered on our behalf. He has become a high priest forever, in the order of Melchizedek.

—HEBREWS 6:13–20

See, when we think of adventure, often times we get thrilling feelings about an exciting life, but adventure often includes danger, risk, frightening situations, and even pain. Think about your favorite adventurer. Was his or her life just simply exciting or did they go through difficult storms, too? Did they suffer? Did they make hard choices? At times did they feel weak or incapable? If they were a true hero or heroine, I'm sure their journeys were not all fun and games.

When we talk about choosing the adventurous life over the reckless existence or the life characterized by playing it safe, one must expect that the life which makes a difference will include pain, challenge, and sacrifice. Consider Jesus. He arguably lived the greatest adventure of anyone in the history of the world. His life on earth included beautiful and amazing episodes of miracles, healings, forgiveness, restorations of dignity for people and loving friendship, but it also included pain, rejection, and ultimately giving up His life on the cross. This adventure does not just cost a few things here and there—it costs everything! The beautiful paradox found in life within relationship with our extravagantly loving God is that when you give up everything—your life—you gain Him Who is eternal, abundant life!

When you choose this adventure you are equipped with everything needed. God—the Father, Son, and the Holy Spirit accompany us in every moment. He is our compass, our light, our life vest, our sails, and certainly our anchor. God is our love, joy, peace, and hope.

I headed to a tattoo shop a couple of months after surgery. To celebrate this gift of healing I got the word "hope" tattooed on my not so impressive bicep (although I think the tattoo makes it a bit more impressive). I felt changed. I felt radical. Whatever was happening on the inside of me, I wanted to express it outwardly too.

We are all prone to letting situations take control of thoughts and emotions. It is not uncommon for us to feel overwhelmed by the various trials and struggles that come our way. Family problems, financial difficulties, emotional hurts, physical pain, and so much more can get in the way of us seeing Jesus. But we cannot adventure without Him. Our intimate worship of Him brings fresh revelation of His good character which gives us hope and builds our faith. This gets us through all the struggles and trials. He is the only real hope, the One who is an anchor for our soul.

Reflection

1. Are you going through a season of pain or trial? How does God want to draw you closer to Him in this time? What does He want you to experience in relationship with him?

2. Worship often leads to intimacy, which leads to deeper revelation of God's nature. In this time, how can you develop a heart that loves to worship?

3. Are their aspects of the Holy Spirit that you do not understand or are even scared of? Where do your fears come from?

Meditation

Look up verses about the Holy Spirit. Here are some to get you started:

- Matthew 3:11; 10:20

- Luke 11:13

- John 7:38–39; 14:26; 15:26; 16:13–14

- Acts 1:8; 2:1–21; 4:31

- Romans 5:5; 8:11–17; 8:26–27

- 1 Corinthians 2:4, 10; 6:11, 19–20; all of chapter 12

Ask the Holy Spirit to give you new revelation as you explore the scriptures. Ask for the fullness of His love, power, authority, and comfort.

NOTES

CHAPTER 13

❖

Finding Shelter and Being a Shelter

At the beginning of 2014, I asked our Heavenly Father for direction for the new year that I was about to embark on. He spoke clearly to my spirit, "Build a sanctuary for the Holy Spirit in your home." This word did not mean we were to change anything about the physical layout of our house, or even that we were to manage it differently. This was a reminder that my family was called to be a sanctuary to those within and outside of God's family. Rick, Grady, Han, Judah and I are all priests (according to 1 Peter 2:9) given permission to enter the sweet presence of our God. And not only did we have the authority to enter into His presence, we have received a beautiful gift, the opportunity to draw others into this sweet presence. We were given His beautiful presence to experience the extravagant love of our Savior, and we were now equipped to serve as a sanctuary for others on their journeys.

One of the most valuable lessons learned in adventuring with the Holy Spirit in my twenties is that rest is always available in this sanctuary. Even with major life changes—like going from zero to two children in a nine-month period, or encountering very challenging people and situations at work, there was never a moment where I could not lean back and trust in His goodness, savor His joy, embrace His hope, and enjoy the closeness of relationships with dear brothers and sisters.

This rest comes from the Holy Spirit, yet He uses His people, His church, to be agents of this rest. And while so many of us can accept that the Spirit of our living God brings beautiful refreshing love, joy, peace, and hope in our lives, we still have a hard time seeing how this happens through God's people. We often do not trust people. We keep our walls up. We deny ourselves the very thing God wants to use to draw us closer to Him—a community of believers.

My generation has a lot of skepticism and fears about church, a lot of baggage and pain caused by those who have professed to be believers in Jesus, but do not live like it. Yet we are all still longing for close community. I loved my church family growing up. But in college, I gave up on the idea of church, because I gave up on people. I looked at all the crazy, loveless, religious nuts in the spotlight or in my Facebook news feed, and believed this lie that everyone was either too religious or too apathetic for the church to have any kind of effectiveness in our world. I was hurt. I was ashamed by those saying they believed in Christ but did nothing to bring good news to anyone. I let pride take over, and suddenly I thought I did not need the Body of Christ. I thought as one individual Christian, I could go it alone.

But when Rick and I started going to our church, United

Assembly, the Lord did some major work on my heart and mind. I grew to love United, with all its quirks, with all its oddballs, with all its openness to the move of the Spirit, and with all its imperfections. And this was largely because I loved the people, even the ones with whom I had little in common. United Assembly became a beautiful sanctuary for me, too. I could experience the sweet presence of God there, just as I could outside by a fire or inside our home's "upper room."

As I grew to love the ones I worshipped and served with, I began to see again why the church is called the body of Christ, needing every part to function at its highest capacity. Could I serve God with just my own family? Of course—but our service alone is limited. There is an abundance of purposeful reasons to serve with a much larger, more diverse group. We need a whole church to reach a whole world. At some point we have to lay down the prideful notion that everyone except us is really a giant hypocrite and begin to function together as a family who is all about reconciling our missing members.

Praying for my church family one night, I received a vision from the Holy Spirit. In this vision, my co-laboring brothers and sisters were all gathered around in an airplane hangar, and Jesus was placing parachutes on each of us. When Jesus placed a pack on an individual, all the others of us gathered together around the one who just received the pack to make sure the straps of the parachutes were securely fastened.

The church is not just a place where we find sanctuary; it is a place where we are launched out into the world to serve as sanctuaries. We come into a community of believers to experience true family. This spiritual family is not without fault or conflict or failure. These are real relationships with real joy and real suffering. But despite the imperfections this is a place where we learn to truly hear, see, and obey our Heavenly Father. We realize that it has been a lie that we could do this on our own because the body needs all its parts.

> *Just as a body, though one, has many parts, but all its many parts form one body, so it is with Christ. For we were all baptized by one Spirit so as to form one body—whether Jews or Gentiles, slave or free—and we were all given the one Spirit to drink. Even so the body is not made up of one part but of many.*
>
> *Now if the foot should say, "Because I am not a hand, I do not belong to the body," it would not for that reason stop being part of the body. And if the ear should say, "Because I am not an eye, I do not belong to the body," it would not for that reason stop being part of the body. If the whole body were an eye, where would the sense of hearing be? If the whole body were an ear, where would the sense of smell be? But in fact God has placed the parts in the body, every one of them, just as he wanted them to be. If they were all one part, where would the body be? As it is, there are many parts, but one body.*
>
> —1 CORINTHIANS 12:12–20

We need every member of the body. Just as we need every member, we need to recognize that our unique part is needed as well. We don't need to be jealous of another member's gifts—

we should be thankful for them. When we value our uniqueness and the uniqueness of our fellow brothers and sisters we really begin to function well. We become a launching pad—launching members into service, and at the same time we become the sanctuary taking care of the members. We support others as they minister according to their gifts, and we receive the support we need to effectively use our own gifts. Sanctuaries and launching pads have two very different purposes, yet the church is both. Sanctuaries are a safe refuge, while launching pads thrust us into thrilling adventure. The beautiful paradox within the Christian community is that when we are safe and secure in the love of our Heavenly Father and our brothers and sisters, we are ready to be brave. We are protected by that love even on rescue missions in the darkest places. We remember that nothing separates us from the love of God—not even death.

When our Creator formed us, He put dreams and passion in us to strategically create Kingdom culture here on earth. While we might live some of those things out alone, we were created to be a part of a much bigger family, a much more complete picture of His plan to rescue the lost, heal the sick, and restore the broken-hearted.

The more I functioned within a community of believers, the more I discovered the dreams and passion my Heavenly Father placed within me. I realized that working as college administrator was not my deepest longing. I had always felt a pull to pursue justice for those suffering the worst kind of injustices. This is why in my earlier years I wanted to become a lawyer, so I could defend the defenseless. I started to long for a change.

I dreamed of other jobs that would employ more of my gifts. And when I grew weary of waiting for a new opportunity, my church family gave me hope. They listened to me when I needed to cry. They supported me through prayer. They loved me regardless of my attitude. When I had moments of doubting God's goodness, they reminded me of that extravagant love He has always shown me.

After about six months of praying for a new ministry opportunity, I had an interesting interaction with one of my students. During class I had my students practice "soaking" as a way to relieve stress. Remember, soaking means to simply rest in the presence of the Lord. After class one of my students came up to me and asked if I had been frustrated with my job lately.

"Uhhhhh…" I stammered. I could not confess that to a student, could I?

He began again, "I think the Lord wants to tell you to 'Hold on.'"

I thanked him and told him his word was very timely. I wrote those two words down. Hold on.

I rested in knowing that God would never forget my current frustrations, and that He had something in store for me that even I could not imagine. I would not know the details of the opportunity before my thirtieth birthday. At twenty-nine I was on the edge of my seat, waiting, often impatiently for the next season. I did not know exactly what or when this change would happen, but I rested in the knowledge of my Heavenly Father's goodness and enjoyed the comfort of my church family.

When Jesus ascended into heaven, He did not leave the earth void of His powerful presence. When He died the veil separating the ordinary people from His residing place, the Holy of Holies, tore in two from top to bottom. A few days after Jesus' departure, a Counselor just like Him came to be with us. Jesus blessed us with the Holy Spirit so all men and all women could become temples, dwelling places for the Most High God. Rather than visit a place of His presence and power from time to time, His presence and power now lives within every believer. That power is a gift to individuals and the entire Body of Christ.

My husband has been given the gift of generosity. Not many believers I've met have this gift as strongly as Rick does. He loves to bless people through giving of time, money, and other resources. When our oldest son Grady was just three we were coming home from a birthday party, and I could tell Rick was deep in thought. Rick said he was thinking about how when God is generous to us it is both because He delights in giving us good gifts, and He enables us to bless others. Rick went on to say that he wanted to always buy two of whatever our children really wanted for their birthdays. One would be for them to keep and one would be for them to give away. This would be just one small way to demonstrate to them how generous our Heavenly Father is.

In God's Kingdom, His gifts to us are beneficial to us and to others. When He is generous to us, it transforms us, increasing our ability to be generous with others. When He shows us mercy, we are empowered to be merciful to others. When He creates a sanctuary for us, we then get to provide a sanctuary for others. Likewise, when He rescues us, He commissions us to rescue others. This is the ministry of reconciliation. First Christ rescues us and then He calls us to help Him rescue our lost brothers and sisters, welcoming them into the family of God.

But we are not ready for the ministry of reconciliation until we receive the full equipping of the Holy Spirit, a gift from our Savior Jesus. A church without the power of the Holy Spirit is only capable of functioning in natural human strength. The power that the Holy Spirit gives us takes us beyond our own natural talents and strengths. The supernatural gifts He gives us reflect and reveal our supernatural God. Only a Spirit-filled and Spirit-led church can change the world. When the community of likeminded believers embraces and functions in the gifts available from the Holy Spirit, the whole church is ready to reach a whole world.

Now you are the body of Christ, and each one of you is a part of it. And God has placed in the church first of all apostles, second prophets, third teachers, then miracles, then gifts of healing, of helping, of guidance, and of different kinds of tongues. Are all apostles? Are all prophets? Are all teachers? Do all work miracles? Do all have gifts of healing? Do all speak in tongues? Do all interpret? Now eagerly desire the greater gifts.

—1 CORINTHIANS 12: 27–31

On this adventure the church is like our airplane hangar, and the Holy Spirit is our parachute. We need both for a successful jump. The Holy Spirit is enough to direct, empower and equip us, but the church is meant to help each member become a minister. We are more effective when we work together. When we have men and women, scholars and craftsmen, every tribe and tongue, realists and idealists and artisans and guardians, when the body has all of its parts we function as we were meant to. His Spirit provides each one of us shelter in His love. And when we come together as the family of God, we become a shelter for all those around us.

Reflection

1. What are your current thoughts and feelings towards the church? What experiences have influenced your current attitude toward community and corporate ministry?

2. How could a local church benefit from the gifts God has given you? How could you be a more effective agent of reconciliation if working with a community of believers?

3. What individuals or groups do you feel called to shelter or protect? Do you know of any churches already serving these populations?

Meditation

Re-read 1 Corinthians 12 and consider your own natural talents, supernatural gifts, and strengths. If you are not sure, pray and ask Holy Spirit to tell you more about how you've been specifically created to make the Body of Christ stronger.

NOTES

CHAPTER 14

Bridge Day

One night, after leading my weekly late night campus Bible study, I felt my Heavenly Father prompting me to journal about significant occurrences in my twenties. I wrote down about fifteen things, such as some of my undergraduate experiences, trips abroad, my marriage to Rick and the addition of my children, Grady and Hananiah. Then I felt Holy Spirit invite me to dream about my thirties. As I neared the end of my twenty-ninth year on this earth, He prompted, "What do you want to do together next?"

Very quickly I jotted down that I wanted to add two more children to our family of four, one through the miracle of childbirth and one through the gift of adoption. I wrote down that I wanted to go the extra six miles and run an ultra-marathon, and that I wanted to write a book. And then out of nowhere *India* came from the ink in my pen. I did not know why. I had never been anywhere in Asia or the Middle East. I did not speak Hindi or know much about Hinduism. But I could not escape this thought, desire even, for India to be a part of the next decade of my life.

Over the next few months, something strange began to happen. Everywhere I went I saw people from India, heard stories about people going to India, and met people who had connections to India. Finally, after hearing in one of our university chapel services about a beautiful church planting movement in India, I thought I needed to look into how I might go to this foreign land.

My dad's ministry, The Mordecai Project, sponsors a home for girls who have been abandoned in Tanuku, India, so I thought my first step would be to check his ministry schedule. Perhaps I could travel with him if he had a trip scheduled. As soon as I got to a computer I checked and could not believe what I found. My dad had a trip to India scheduled and he would be there on my thirtieth birthday! The Holy Spirit again reminded me that this was an opportunity to do something special with Him for the Kingdom. I was super excited about the prospect of going, but one thing concerned me. On my thirtieth birthday, I would also be twenty-one weeks pregnant.

I researched pregnancy and travel, and concluded somewhat soundly that it would be safe to go. I did have a few concerns, one being that I might be at risk for typhoid. Little research had been done on this vaccination and its impact on a fetus, so I elected to just be extremely cautious about what I ate and drank after consulting with my midwife and a travel clinic nurse. I was ninety-five percent excited and ready, and about five percent terrified about taking this mission trip with my unborn baby.

Two weeks before my departure, Rick and I had a fetal anatomy scan appointment with my doctor's office. I did not dare let myself hope for a daughter. I always knew I wanted a daughter, but after welcoming two sons to the family, I convinced myself that I could still be happy and satisfied with a pack of little boys. I told myself it was utterly pointless to hope for something already determined. I know I would have been happy with another son. I was expecting another son. I even had a name picked out for the next Turner boy.

When the ultrasound technician first showed us the little one inside me, we all cooed over the fact that the baby's ankles were crossed and had hands resting on face. I immediately said, "Awe she's…I mean it's so cute!" The technician asked if I already knew the gender and Rick and I both said, "No". We proceeded to see the arms, legs, face and then the technician said, "You were right mom. It's a she." And immediately tears of joy started streaming down my face.

Quite suddenly I did not want to go to India. Now that I could see her, the reality of the precious gift became quite overwhelming. I knew I could not put her in harm's way. I could not take a risk that could hurt her. I did not know what to do. I had paid almost two thousand dollars for a plane ticket. I had a travel companion depending on me. But I did not care about that. I now doubted this profound adventure that lay before me. I did not want to be brave—I wanted to play it safe. My new found resistance was not Spirt-led discernment. It was genuine, human fear.

But the Holy Spirit graciously removed my doubts about His calling me to go. I let the anxiety go. Through a work only He could do, He affirmed His calling and rejuvenated my excitement for the trip.

Our primary ministry in India was to serve thirty-three young girls living in a home sponsored by The Mordecai Project, (see: http://www.themordecaiproject.org/welcome/) a ministry that empowers and protects women all over Africa, South America, and Asia. Some of these little girls were left to die in trash cans. All of them were given up because of one simple fact—they were daughters, not sons.

In India, it is illegal for a doctor to tell parents if their unborn child is a boy or a girl. The government fears greatly that little girls will be aborted in mass if this kind of information was released. This is the sad reality that little girls all over the world live in. The day of their birth meant sorrow, because baby girls are not valued by many.

How profound it was to stand before them and tell them how I had longed for a little girl and that God had given me one of the deepest desires of my heart. I told them our Heavenly Father loves His daughters just as much as He loves His sons. I told them that He delights in them, the way I will delight in my little girl. I told them they were precious to Him, simply because they were His baby girls.

In that moment I could barely fathom the depths, the beauty, the significance of this partnership with Christ. I could not have made this story up. He orchestrated this beautiful moment to give hope and love to these thirty-three young girls, and He picked me and my daughter, Judah, to be a part of the story.

And so it is with each of us. When we submit ourselves to the leading of the Holy Spirit, when we choose bravery over safety, and when we embark on this journey with Christ, our lives tell a beautiful story of the goodness of God.

I had my thirtieth birthday the day we left India. My feet touched three continents in one day that lasted over thirty hours. As we flew back in time across the time zones towards home, I reflected on the past decade of my life. I did not have profound regrets. I felt both a sense of satisfaction and yearning. I was so grateful for all the stories, all the adventures of the past, but I also knew the best was yet to come.

I wonder how many individuals, on the eve of their thirtieth birthday, desire to go back in time and start over? I think that for those who are prone to treating their twenties like an extended adolescence or some weird throw away period there might be a great deal of sadness, dissatisfaction and even regret as they reflect back on a lost decade so full of wasted potential.

I want to encourage those just leaving home, those just starting college, the ones just starting these twenty-somethings years. I want to reiterate some really important things to encourage you.

Begin this adventure by developing your own real relationship with your Heavenly Father, be reconciled through Jesus and be filled with the Holy Spirit.

Change your major to something you are really interested in, no matter what others think. Value your education and be very grateful for the privilege to work hard to earn a degree.

Don't marry just anybody because you're afraid you'll be

alone if you don't rush to meet some imaginary deadline.

Go on that overseas mission trip or take that crazy internship. Apply for that dream job, or volunteer with that non-profit even when you know the challenges that will come with the opportunity.

Commit to your community even when it is hard. Love people and love the church, even when they offend and hurt. Be a part of a reconciliation movement, not an I-can-do-this-on my-own movement.

Last of all, I want to say something much more simple, but much more meaningful. To those beginning this leap from adolescence to adulthood, *be brave!* Any decision made out of fear is not a decision guided by the Holy Spirit. The Holy Spirit makes us strong and fearless.

> *For this reason I remind you to fan into flame the gift of God, which is in you through the laying on of my hands. For the Spirit God gave us does not make us timid, but gives us power, love and self-discipline. So do not be ashamed of the testimony about our Lord or of me his prisoner. Rather, join with me in suffering for the gospel, by the power of God. He has saved us and called us to a holy life—not because of anything we have done but because of his own purpose and grace. This grace was given us in Christ Jesus before the beginning of time, but it has now been revealed through the appearing of our Savior, Christ Jesus, who has destroyed death and has brought life and immortality to light through the gospel.*

> —2 TIMOTHY 1:6–10

We serve a God who destroyed death. We submit our lives to a God who loved us so much that He was compelled to reach us with the fullness of His light and abundant life. He was not content to leave us in a state of slavery to a sinful condition and fallen world. His desire is that we actually live out heavenly realities in our earth realms, that we reconcile everything back to His love and grace. Boredom, complacency, fear, and monotony are not in the cards for us when we choose to live the adventure with Him.

Back in 2004 when I rafted the Gauley River with Rick, we experienced quite a sight. We were there on what is known as Bridge Day, when hundreds of people gather to BASE jump (parachute from a fixed structure) off the New River Bridge. This bridge is one of the highest in the nation. And beneath the bridge are the raging rapids! Those who gather on that bridge know in theory what their journey risks. There is a danger in leaping away from the man made structure, and there is desperate hope that one's parachute will really open and guide the jumper on this exhilarating ride. But what they can't know until they leap away is the exhilaration, the blissful rush of the free fall.

And so it should be with us. When Christ beckons us to follow him, we should calculate the natural risk and embrace the supernatural hope. We should rejoice in the life joined with our Savior, not because it is without danger or suffering. We know to expect such things. But we rejoice because this life is what we were meant for. We can evade the opportunity, but the opportunity cannot evade us. So I hope that you choose to jump into the adventure God has for you. Let go of your fear and doubt. Follow Him, the one who loves you so extravagantly. He wants your story to be beautiful and full of meaning. My prayer is that we all point others to this extravagant love as we embark on the adventure available in every moment with Him. Happy jumping.

Reflection

1. On the eve of your thirtieth birthday, what do you hope to have experienced or accomplished? If you are already past thirty, what about the decades to follow?

2. What choices are you making today that will propel you to be where you want in the future?

3. Are there fears you need to let go of to live bravely with Christ? What are they?

Meditation

Re-read the passage in 2 Timothy. Think about any fears or anxiety in your life and ask Holy Spirit to replace that fear with love, power, and self-discipline. Journal about the fears you are surrendering and the specific adventures you want to be empowered for.

NOTES

ADVENTURE AVAILABLE

Made in the USA
Middletown, DE
17 October 2016